PRAYERS FOR
URGENT OCCASIONS

JESUS: OUR CONSOLER — "Come to me, all you who labor and are burdened, and I will give you rest."—Mt 11:28f

Prayers

for

Urgent Occasions

Texts Chosen, Translated, and Annotated

By
Rev. Bernard-Marie, O.F.S.
Doctor of Theology

Illustrated

CATHOLIC BOOK PUBLISHING CO.
New York

NIHIL OBSTAT: John Quinn, M.A.
Censor Librorum

IMPRIMATUR: Patrick J. Sheridan
Vicar General, Archdiocese of New York

This book was originally published in French by Editions du Chalet, Paris, under the title *Prières pour les causes difficiles ou désespérées*. The English translation is by Anthony M. Buono.

(T-918)

CONTENTS

5

INTRODUCTION

In the following pages the reader will find an ensemble of texts grouped generally according to the order of classical theology. * They are therefore addressed first to God, then to the Blessed Virgin Mary, next to the Angels and Saints, and finally to the holy souls in purgatory, whose powerful intercession should not be neglected.

Obviously, these texts are not to be recited at one time. Moreover, it would be more in keeping with a sane approach to follow as much as possible the order of the book by drawing, for example, a prayer from each of the categories. Running directly to St. Rita without even placing oneself in the presence of God and greeting the Ruler of the world would be tantamount to passing before an illustrious king without looking at him and having eyes only for his lowly attendant. Do we really believe that the attendant would be pleased that his

---

* Especially beginning with chapter 3, many of the texts cited are the original prayers of the author. Others are the reprise of known texts that have been extensively revised to make them briefer, more Biblical, and more open to the communitary ecclesial perspective. At the same time, all the spiritual riches of these classical texts (such as the prayers of St. Bridget) have been carefully preserved.

king was ignored? Do we seriously think that a king would favorably receive the pleas of impolite subjects who were too occupied with themselves and so little attentive to the true values of things?

Therefore, we must never fail to take a brief moment to place ourselves with all our heart in the presence of the heavenly King—to greet Him and tell Him of our trusting love, our wretchedness, and our need to be saved by His all-powerful grace. This gratuitous prayer will lead us to do the will of God and give us the strength to accept it if in the last analysis Divine Providence chooses to answer our prayer in a manner other than the one we originally intended.

Certainly, to greet the most high King is already something good, but we must not do so clothed in rags and without being purified in body and spirit. If we want God to hear and answer us favorably, we must seek to be pleasing to Him. If we have sinned gravely, we must repent sincerely, make reparation for the wrong we have done, and as soon as possible receive the Sacrament of Confession. Only then should we come to present our petitions to Almighty God.

If, on the other hand, we believe that we are just and are conscious of no serious sin, we must recall the humility of the Saints and not hesitate to entrust to God our weakness that is continually menaced by temptations and falls. If Jesus was tempted by the devil in the desert and underwent his assaults in Gethsemane, His friends will experience a similar fate: "No slave is greater than his master" (Jn 15:20).

Above all, we must tell God again of our faith and unfailing hope despite all appearances. We must firmly resist all tendency to despair or to rebel in the face of the injustice (often so great) of this world. We must offer the Lord our wounded heart in union with the Heart of Jesus crucified. We must rather look at the Cross of salvation and hear the words of the Risen One: "Take courage, I have conquered the world" (Jn 16:33).

The more desperate is our cause, the more it will be necessary to draw to our side all that is Christianly possible to obtain the miracle that we seek. We should therefore make use of meditation and put into practice the following ten points, taking care not to exclude any of them for they are organically linked in the faith.

1) First examine if the grace requested proceeds from a pure intention and is in accord with the spirit of the Gospel (see Mt 5:3-48). In case of doubt, have recourse to a priest or a consecrated person.

2) Make a commitment to lead a more saintly life and offer sacrifices for the spiritual good of the person or persons for whom we pray (child, adult, aged person).

3) Show more faith and perseverance in prayer, after the example of our Lord Who often prolonged His prayer into the night (see Lk 6:12; Mt 14:23). If, for example, we have chosen to make a novena, it is necessary to carry out all the exercises indicated and without interruption for nine consecutive days.

Afterward, we can rest in peace in the knowledge that sometimes God hears us *by stages* to respect certain spiritual, biological, and psychological processes that take time. At times, he also answers us only *partially* so as to sustain our hope yet not completely eliminate our participation in the saving Cross.

4) Do not hesitate to invite other believers to join in some of your prayers, for the Lord more easily grants His graces to those who come together in His name with faith

and generosity (see Mt 18:20). This has been well understood by members of the little prayer groups that have issued from the Charismatic Renewal.*

5) Think of having the Eucharist celebrated often for the person or persons for whom we ask a grace. Go to pray for them at the church, before the Blessed Sacrament, even if it be only for a few minutes.

6) As often as possible receive Communion and not only honor God and the Blessed Virgin Mary but also recommend yourself to the Saint of the day. Then confide in him or her the difficult thing for which you pray. On the day the Church celebrates his or her feast a Saint can obtain for us a very particular grace, but we must ask it of him or her.

7) If the sickness or the advancing years begin to weigh more heavily on the person for whom you pray, do not hesitate to suggest that he or she receive the Sacrament of the Anointing of the Sick. Not only will this be spiritually salutary for the

---

* Some of them have also specialized in what they call "the prayer of intercession" for every form of spiritual and corporal healing. This refers manifestly to the ministry of healing of which St. Paul speaks in 1 Corinthians 12:9, 28.

recipient but it may also bring about the renewal of bodily health (see Jas 5:15).

8) Know how to use with discernment and discretion the various devotions and sacramentals that the Church puts at our disposal: Rosary, Stations of the Cross, pilgrimages, wearing of a cross or a scapular, offering of a candle or flowers, blessing with holy water, absorption of water from Lourdes with the sentiments required by the Church, imposition of relics,* or the wearing of a blessed medal recommended by the Church, for example, the one known as the "Miraculous Medal." In 1830, the Blessed Virgin Mary revealed to St. Margaret Mary Alacoque that "the persons who wear this medal and say with de-

---

*This term refers to all that a Saint leaves behind after death: body, instrument of martyrdom, objects belonging to him or her. The Church can offer certain of them for our veneration, for they were the remote or proximate material instruments of the sanctification of this Saint and the visible channels by which graces were transmitted to human beings. It is a fact attested by the whole history of the Church that certain authentic cures were obtained through the imposition of holy relics. However, in this area we must as always avoid all idea of magic in the granting of prayers. We must rather recall that God sometimes performs a miracle not because of the relics themselves but because of the faith of the believers on the one hand and the merits of the Saint on the other.

votion every day the invocation 'O Mary conceived without sin, pray for us who have recourse to you' will enjoy a very special protection.'"

9) Even if God does not answer you as you hoped, know how to abandon yourself to His holy will, like Jesus at Gethsemane: "Father, . . . not what I will but what you will" (Mk 14:36). If we undergo the trial with these sentiments of filial abandonment, there is no doubt that the Father, as He did for Jesus (see Lk 22:43), will send His Angel of consolation who will strengthen us. Therefore, we should rely on His Word full of treasures that are always disposable and actual. We should often open the Gospel, that "other ciborium of God."

10) Finally, dare to believe in God to such an extent as to give Him thanks for all His designs, even the most mysterious and crucifying. Certainly, sin and death seem at times to cruelly triumph, but since the Paschal Resurrection of Christ, the Cross—while still remaining a Cross—has become luminous and the bearer of an inextinguishable hope. Ever since Easter and the effusion of the Holy Spirit at Pentecost, everything has become possible, including the conversion of hearts of stone and the rever-

sal of seemingly difficult or quasi-desperate situations.

The reason for this is because it is the Holy Spirit Himself Who comes to pray and supplicate the Father in us (see Rom 8:26). Not only does He assume our humble prayer but He also carries us further along the road of faith and reveals to us what we can now fittingly ask of God in order to be pleasing to Him and be heard.

In concluding, let me remind you that there is a *Thematic Table of Intentions* at the end of this volume. At least at the beginning, this will aid you to find the most appropriate approach for your situation. Nevertheless, if time permits, you will gain much by meditating on all the prayers in this book. They form a whole, a "theology on one's knees," in which all the parts act like the cells of a single body.

The author wishes to thank all those who have helped him to conceive and to compose this work, notably his religious librarian friends and Father Jean Evenou who offered very useful liturgical advice.

THE TRINITY: ONE GOD IN THREE PERSONS
— Our prayer life should manifest the fact that
the Blessed Trinity constitutes the central real-
ity for Christians. Our entire lives are lived in
the loving embrace of Father, Son, and Holy
Spirit.

18

1. PRAYERS TO GOD

THE CELEBRATION OF
THE EUCHARIST

The Celebration of the Eucharist is at the source and at the summit of every grace. In a mysterious but very real way it actualizes the saving offering of Christ on Calvary, and through Communion it gives us the very Author of grace, the Risen Jesus, true God and true Man.

Remember that we can always have a Mass celebrated for the intentions of a particular person, even a living one, especially if he or she is in great moral and spiritual difficulty.

Since it is the greatest prayer, the Mass must become a quasi-daily necessity for us.

THE PSALMS OF SUPPLICATION

Especially when we are suffering anguish and evil, we should often pray with the texts of the Psalms of Supplication. They served Christ, Mary, and the first Christians in expressing their most ardent desires to the heavenly Father. In addition, all these Psalms are found in the Liturgy of the Hours, which has been recited for centuries by all priests and consecrated souls who thus pray for the needs of the world. The recitation of any of these Psalms will aid our prayer to become more Catholic, that is, more universal.

Psalm 22

My God, my God, why have you forsaken
    me,
  far from my prayer, from the words of
    my cry?
O my God, I cry out by day, and you an-
    swer not;
  by night, and there is no relief for me.

Yet you are enthroned in the holy place,
  O glory of Israel!
In you our fathers trusted;
  they trusted, and you delivered them.
To you they cried, and they escaped;
  in you they trusted, and they were not
    put to shame.

But I am a worm, not a man;
  the scorn of men, despised by the people.
All who see me scoff at me;
  they mock me with parted lips, they wag
    their heads:
"He relied on the Lord; let him deliver him,
  let him rescue him, if he loves him."

You have been my guide since I was first
    formed,
  my security at my mother's breast.

To you I was committed at birth,
    from my mother's womb you are my
      God.

Be not far from me, for I am in distress;
    be near, for I have no one to help
      me. . . .
I am like water poured out;
    all my bones are racked.

My heart has become like wax
    melting away within my bosom.
My throat is dried up like baked clay,
    my tongue cleaves to my jaws;
    to the dust of death you have brought me
      down.

Indeed, many dogs surround me,
    a pack of evildoers closes in upon me;
They have pierced my hands and my feet;
    I can count all my bones.

They look on and gloat over me;
    they divide my garments among them,
    and for my vesture they cast lots.

But you, O Lord, be not far from me;
    O my help, hasten to aid me. . . .

Psalm 130

Out of the depths I cry to you, O Lord;
  Lord, hear my voice!
Let your ears be attentive
  to my voice in supplication:

If you, O Lord, mark iniquities,
  Lord, who can stand?
But with you is forgiveness,
  that you may be revered.

I trust in the Lord;
  my soul trusts in his word.
My soul waits for the Lord
  more than sentinels wait for the dawn.

More than sentinels wait for the dawn,
  let Israel wait for the Lord,
For with the Lord is kindness
  and with him is plenteous redemption;
And he will redeem Israel
  from all their iniquities.

Psalm 13

How long, O Lord? Will you utterly forget
    me?
  How long will you hide your face from
    me?

How long shall I harbor sorrow in my soul,
  grief in my heart day after day?

How long will my enemy triumph over me
  Look, answer me, O Lord, my God!

Give light to my eyes that I may not sleep
    in death
  lest my enemy say, "I have overcome
    him";
Lest my foes rejoice at my downfall
  though I trusted in your kindness.

Let my heart rejoice in your salvation;
  let me sing of the Lord, "He has been
    good to me."

Psalm 25

To you I lift up my soul,
  O Lord, my God.
In you I trust; let me not be put to shame,
  let not my enemies exult over me.

No one who waits for you shall be put to
    shame;
  those shall be put to shame who heed-
    lessly break faith.

Your ways, O Lord, make known to me;
  teach me your paths,
Guide me in your truth and teach me,
  for you are God my savior,
  and for you I wait all the day.

Remember that your compassion, O Lord,
   and your kindness are from of old.
The sins of my youth and my frailties remember not;
   in your kindness remember me,
   because of your goodness, O Lord. . . .

All the paths of the Lord are kindness and
   constancy
   toward those who keep his covenant and
   his decrees.
For your name's sake, O Lord,
   you will pardon my guilt, great as it
   is. . . .

My eyes are ever toward the Lord,
   for he will free my feet from the snare.
Look toward me, and have pity on me,
   for I am alone and afflicted.

Relieve the troubles of my heart,
   and bring me out of my distress.
Put an end to my affliction and my suffering,
   and take away all my sins. . . .

Preserve my life, and rescue me;
   let me not be put to shame, for I take refuge in you.
Let integrity and uprightness preserve me,
   because I wait for you, O Lord.

We might also profitably meditate on the following Psalms: 57; 61; 69; 70; 86; 88; 102; 141; 142; 143. This list is not exhaustive.

PRAYER OF JOB,
THE FRIEND OF GOD

Every human being who suffers and encounters the apparent "silence of God" is one with Job, the saintly non-Jewish Biblical personage who belongs to all humankind through the impressive number of his trials. If he never ceases to complain to God, he also never complains about God. His Creator had given him everything; now He has taken away everything from him except his hope. This last legacy is so unforeseen and miraculous, given the circumstances, that we can well cry out with Job himself: "Blessed be the name of the Lord!" (Jb 1:21).

While making some of Job's supplications our own, we should also espouse his unshakable hope, sure sign of the Spirit working in the human heart.

I have no peace nor ease;
  I have no rest, for trouble comes!
                                    Jb 3:26

Oh, that I might have my request,
  and that God would grant what I long
    for.

Jb 6:8

Have I the strength of stones
  or is my flesh of bronze?

Jb 6:12

My soul ebbs away from me;
  days of affliction have overtaken me.

Jb 30:16, 27

I have been assigned months of misery,
  and troubled nights have been told off
    for me.

Jb 7:3

If in bed I say, "When shall I arise?"
  then the night drags on;
  I am filled with restlessness until the
    dawn.

Jb 7:4

What is man, that you make much of him,
  or pay him any heed?

Jb 7:17

Let me know why you oppose me.
  Is it a pleasure for you to oppress?

Jb 10:2-3

Your hands have formed me and fashioned
  me;
  will you then turn and destroy me?

Jb 10:8

I know that I am in the right.
If anyone can make a case against me,
  then I shall be silent and die.

Jb 13:18-19

Why do you hide your face
  and consider me your enemy?

Jb 13:24

My brethren have withdrawn from me,
  and my friends are wholly estranged.

Jb 19:14

Oh, that today I might find him,
  that I might come to his judgment seat!

Jb 23:3

If I go to the east, he is not there;
  or to the west, I cannot perceive him;
Where the north enfolds him, I behold him
  not;
  by the south he is veiled, and I see him
  not.

Jb 23:8-9

God is wise in heart and mighty in
  strength;
  who has withstood him and remained
  unscathed?

Jb 9:4

For God does speak, perhaps once,
　　or even twice, though one perceive it
　　　not.

Jb 33:14

He has decided, and who can say him nay?
　　What he desires, that he does.

Jb 23:13

Lo, God is great beyond our knowledge;
　　the number of his years is past searching
　　　out.

Jb 36:26

The Book of Job ends on a note that shows at what point the hearing of our prayers passes through fraternal forgiveness and the gratuitous intercession for our neighbor.

The Lord restored the prosperity of Job, after he had prayed for his friends.

Job 42:10

PRAYER OF ST. AUGUSTINE

Even if a person should have the very great faith of a Saint doubled by the faith of a Father of the Church, one could still cry out to God his distress and his pressing desire to be saved by God's goodness:

Lord, have pity on me. Alas, You see my wounds, which I do not hide. You are the physician, and I am one who is sick. You are merciful, and I am one who is miserable.

Our life on earth is a warfare! Who would choose trials and difficulties? You command that they should be endured but not that they should be loved. . . .

In adversities I long for prosperities; in prosperities I fear adversities. What middle ground is there between these where our life can be without trial?

Lord, all my hope is only in Your exceedingly great mercy!

St. Augustine, *Confessions*, X, 28-29

ACT OF HOPE

O Lord, trials have turned my life upside down. I do not see clearly along the paths where Your Divine Providence has led me. But I maintain unlimited hope in Your Heart, which is so good and infinitely merciful.

Father Engel, For You Whom Life Has Overcome, p. 150

PRAYER FOR PEACE IN FAMILIES

If the family is sound, everything is sound, or at least everything runs smoother. The family is not only at the basis of every truly human society but also at the root of a child's initial religious sentiments. Therefore, we can never pray too much for the unity and sanctification of families!

O Lord, inspirer of all peace and source of all love, turn Your merciful gaze on our divided family. You desire the unity of hearts, and You are able to mend that unity when it is broken. Have mercy on us.

O Jesus, grant me this grace through Your merits as a most loving and most obedient Son at Nazareth.

O Mary, grant us this grace through your merits as a spouse and most humble and tender Mother at Nazareth.

O St. Joseph, grant us this grace through your merits as spouse and most loving and faithful father at Nazareth.

Glory be to the Father, and to the Son, and to the Holy Spirit. As it was in the beginning, is now, and ever shall be, world without end. Amen.*

---

*Another possible text for the "Glory Be" is: Glory be to the Father, and to the Son, and to the Holy Spirit, to the God Who is, Who was, and Who comes, for ever and ever. Amen.

GOD THE FATHER: OUR CREATOR AND LORD — God the Father is our Creator and Lord as well as our loving Father. Prayer to Him enables us to balance His supreme perfections and transcendence with His loving concern for the slightest thing He has made.

2. PRAYERS TO THE FATHER

THE PRAYER GIVEN US BY JESUS

Our Father, Who art in heaven,
hallowed be Thy Name;
Thy kingdom come;
Thy will be done on earth as it is in heaven.
Give us this day our daily bread;
and forgive us our trespasses
as we forgive those who trespass against us;
and lead us not into temptation,
but deliver us from evil.
For the kingdom, the power, and the glory
   are Yours,
now and forever. (See Mt 6:9-13)

INVOCATION AT THE FOOT
OF THE CROSS

Father of love, do not resist our prayers. Look upon the passion and offering of Your Son Jesus. Listen to Him with His Mother and all Your Church—and have mercy on us!*

---

*This prayer is often said with arms extended as on a cross.

PRAYER OF INTERCESSION
FOR THE DYING

The experience of vigils with the dying has shown us that, recited inwardly with one's whole heart, this prayer for our brothers and sisters suffering death's agony was very often heard and they soon found peace and trustful abandonment to God once again.

Most holy and merciful Father, I offer You the Heart of Your beloved Son with all His love, all His sufferings, and all His merits, in reparation for all the sins committed by N . . . during the course of his/her life up to the present hour of his/her agony. And I implore the Immaculate Virgin herself to bring this sacred offering before You, my God and my Father.

Our Father (p. 33), *Hail Mary* (p. 77), *Glory be to the Father* (p. 31).

Most holy and merciful Father, I offer You the Heart of Your beloved Son with all His love, all His sufferings, and all His merits, to supply the good that N . . . has neglected to accomplish during the course of his/her life up to the present hour of his/

her agony. And I implore the Immaculate Virgin herself to bring this offering before You, my God and my Father. (*Prayers as above.*)

Most holy and merciful Father, I offer You the Heart of Your beloved Son with all His love, all His sufferings, and all His merits, to purify the good that N . . . accomplished during the course of his her life up to the present hour of his her agony. And I implore the Immaculate Virgin herself to bring this offering before You, my God and my Father. (*Prayers as above.*)

GOD THE SON: OUR REDEEMER AND BROTHER — Our knowledge of God is communicated to us primarily by God the Son made Man, Jesus Christ. In Him we have access to the Father. By entrusting ourselves to Him in prayer we attain our true goal in life.

3. PRAYERS TO CHRIST

PRAYERS DRAWN FROM
THE GOSPEL

It is neither the beautiful formulas of our supplications nor their length that touches the Heart of God, but rather the trusting love with which we turn to Him as our unique Savior. In this regard, the Gospel is an excellent model for it gives us the prayers that succeeded in touching Christ and obliging Him, so to speak, to hear us.

We should be ready to draw inspiration from these prayers even today, but without being concerned only with their letter. We should rather strive above all to let the Holy Spirit Who dwells in us express Himself, for He knows what is truly pleasing to the Father of mercies.

"[Lord,] do you not care that we are perishing?"   Mt 4:38

"If you can . . . , have compassion on us and help us."   Mk 9:22

"Lord, save us! We are perishing!"
                                                      Mt 8:25

"Jesus, Master! Have pity on us!"
                          ***   Lk 17:13

"Lord, save me!"   Mt 14:30

"Have pity on me, Lord, Son of David!"
                                    Mt 15:22

"I do believe, help my unbelief!"
                                    Mk 9:24

***

"My daughter is at the point of death. Please, come lay your hands on her that she may get well and live."   Mk 5:23

"[Lord,] I beg you, look at my son; he is my only child."   Lk 9:38

"Master, I want to see."   Mk 10:51

***

"Depart from me, Lord, for I am a sinful man."   Lk 5:8

"My Lord and my God!"   Jn 20:28

"Lord, you know everything; you know that I love you."   Jn 21:17

***

"Master, to whom shall we go? You have the words of eternal life."   Jn 6:68

"Stay with us, for it is nearly evening and the day is almost over."   Lk 24:29

"Jesus, remember me when you come into your kingdom."   Lk 23:42

VARIOUS INVOCATIONS

From all lukewarmness in our faith,
deliver us, Lord Jesus.

From all loss of hope,
deliver us, Lord Jesus.

From all cooling of our love,
deliver us, Lord Jesus.

From all sin and evil
deliver us, Lord Jesus.

From the snares of the devil,
deliver us, Lord Jesus.

From anger and hatred,
deliver us, Lord Jesus.

From all bad faith and evil will,
deliver us, Lord Jesus.

From all despair and morbid folly,
deliver us, Lord Jesus.

From all wretchedness that distances us
from you,
deliver us, Lord Jesus.

From all war and natural calamities,
deliver us, Lord Jesus.

From death in the state of grave sin,
deliver us, Lord Jesus.

From all that can be a cause of sin or scan-
    dal for our neighbor,
deliver us, Lord Jesus.

By your Incarnation and Nativity,
deliver us, Lord Jesus.

By your Baptism and Fast in the desert,
deliver us, Lord Jesus.

By your Sufferings and your Cross,
deliver us, Lord Jesus.

By your Death and Burial,
deliver us, Lord Jesus.

By your holy Resurrection,
deliver us, Lord Jesus.

By your admirable Ascension,
deliver us, Lord Jesus.

By the sending of the Holy Spirit,
deliver us, Lord Jesus.

By your Return in glory,
deliver us, Lord Jesus.

ROSARY OF THE DIVINE MERCY

The Rosary of the Divine Mercy is recited on an ordinary rosary. We can say it preferably for the great intentions of the Church and the world: the unity of Christians, the conversion of sinners, the return of a nation to God, peace among human beings, and the like.

On the single bead, say:

Holy Father, I offer You the Body and Blood, Soul and Divinity of Your Son Jesus in reparation for our sins and the sins of the whole world.

On each of the ten beads (decade), say:

By His sorrowful Passion, have pity on us and on the whole world.

At the end of each decade, say:

Holy God, mighty God, eternal God, have mercy on us.

At the end of the rosary, say:

Blood and water that issued from the Heart of Jesus as the Source of mercy for us, I put my trust in you.

NOVENA OF TRUST IN THE HEART OF CHRIST

This prayer should be said on nine consecutive days, if possible before or after Mass.*

O Jesus, I entrust to Your Heart *this soul, this intention, this pain, this matter.*

Look, O Lord. Then act in accord with the desire of Your Heart.

Let Your Heart act.
O Jesus, I rely on You.
I put my trust in You.
I abandon myself to You.
I am sure of You.

Sacred Heart of Jesus, I put my trust in You.
Sacred Heart of Jesus, I believe in Your Love for me.
Sacred Heart of Jesus, may Your kingdom come!

---

*We might recall that in the 17th century, Christ appeared to St. Margaret Mary Alacoque and recommended to her the devotion to the Sacred Heart and the practice of Eucharistic Communion every first Friday of the month, if possible for at least nine consecutive months. To those who perform this devotion, Christ promised consolation in their trials and blessings on their enterprises as well as true repentance and special assistance at the hour of death.

LITANY OF THE SACRED HEART
OF JESUS

Lord, have mercy.
Christ, have mercy.
Lord, have mercy.
Christ, hear us.
Christ, graciously hear us.
God, the Father of heaven, *have mercy on
    us.* *

God the Son, Redeemer of the world,
God, the Holy Spirit,
Holy Trinity, one God,
Heart of Jesus, Son of the eternal Father,
Heart of Jesus, formed by the Holy Spirit
    in the womb of the Virgin Mother,
Heart of Jesus, substantially united to the
    Word of God,
Heart of Jesus, of infinite majesty,
Heart of Jesus, sacred temple of God,
Heart of Jesus, tabernacle of the Most
    High,
Heart of Jesus, house of God and gate of
    heaven,
Heart of Jesus, burning furnace of charity,
Heart of Jesus, abode of justice and love,
Heart of Jesus, full of goodness and love,

---

*Have mercy on us *is repeated after each invocation.*

Heart of Jesus, abyss of all virtues,

Heart of Jesus, most worthy of all praise,

Heart of Jesus, king and center of all hearts,

Heart of Jesus, in Whom are all the treasures of wisdom and knowledge,

Heart of Jesus, in Whom dwells the fullness of the Divinity,

Heart of Jesus, in Whom the Father was well pleased,

Heart of Jesus, of Whose fullness we have all received,

Heart of Jesus, desire of the everlasting hills,

Heart of Jesus, patient and most merciful,

Heart of Jesus, enriching all who invoke You,

Heart of Jesus, fountain of life and holiness,

Heart of Jesus, propitiation for our sins,

Heart of Jesus, loaded down with opprobrium,

Heart of Jesus, bruised for our offenses,

Heart of Jesus, obedient to death,

Heart of Jesus, pierced with a lance,

Heart of Jesus, source of all consolation,

Heart of Jesus, our life and resurrection,

Heart of Jesus, our peace and reconciliation,

Heart of Jesus, victim for our sins,

Heart of Jesus, salvation of those who trust in You,

Heart of Jesus, hope of those who die in You,

Heart of Jesus, delight of all the Saints,

Lamb of God, You take away the sins of the world; *spare us, O Lord.*

Lamb of God, You take away the sins of the world; *graciously hear us, O Lord.*

Lamb of God, You take away the sins of the world; *have mercy on us.*

℣. Jesus, meek and humble of Heart.

℟. *Make our hearts like to Yours.*

Let us pray. Almighty and eternal God, look upon the Heart of Your most beloved Son and upon the praise and satisfaction that He offers You in the name of sinners; and to those who implore Your mercy, in Your great goodness, grant forgiveness in the name of the same Jesus Christ, Your Son, Who lives and reigns with You forever and ever. ℟. *Amen.*

THE 15 PRAYERS OF ST. BRIDGET

The fifteen prayers that follow are, according to a tradition that goes back to St. Bridget (14th century), to be recited each day, or at least each Friday, if possible for a year. Those who often make this meditation with faith and devotion will obtain the graces of special assistance at the hour of their death. These same graces could also be given to every person that the supplicants would desire to entrust along with themselves to the mercy of God.

These prayers have been lightly retouched by us so as to enrich them with new Biblical and ecclesial perspectives—but without affecting the traditional riches that they already possessed.

1st Prayer

Praised be You, O Jesus, my Lord, for all the sufferings that You voluntarily accepted to bear for us during Your whole life and especially at the time of Your Passion.

On Holy Thursday, You humbly washed the feet of all Your Apostles, thus leaving them a wonderful example of humility and true spiritual greatness.

At the Paschal repast of the Last Supper, You offered under the species of bread and wine Your own Body and Your own Blood in sacrifice for our sins. Out of love, You gave them as nourishment to Your Apostles, thus preparing them in the best possible way for Your holy Passion that was soon to be accomplished.

In consideration of this total sacrifice of Yourself under a sacramental form, I beg You, my Savior, to purify us from all pride and egotism. Fortified by Your holy Eucharist, may we also follow in Your footsteps and offer our lives for the love of God, the purification of our souls, and the salvation of our brothers and sisters on earth! Amen.

Our Father, Hail Mary, Glory be to the Father.

2nd Prayer

In the Garden of Gethsemane, You confided in Your three disciples Peter, James, and John: "My soul is sorrowful even to death" (Mt 26:38). So great was Your anguish that a bloody sweat issued from Your innocent Body. Yet You lovingly willed to accomplish to the end our redemption, praying thus: "Father, . . . not my will but yours be done" (Lk 22:42).

In consideration of that horrible agony of soul, I beg You, my Savior, to make us worthy to live our last moments in conformity with the will of God and after Your example. Purify us, protect us, and lead us without hindrance to Your most holy Father. Yes, we wish to obey His loving will, no matter what it costs, but stay with us always, most sweet and merciful Lord Jesus! Amen.

Our Father, Hail Mary, Glory be to the Father.

3rd Prayer

Praised be You, O Jesus, my Savior, for humbly accepting to be interrogated by Caiaphas and submitting to the judgment of Pilate, even though You are the Judge of all!

In consideration of Your sublime willingness to be so misunderstood by the leaders and teachers of Your day, I ask You, my Savior, to preserve forever in us a child's heart. For it is to children and those who resemble them that Your heavenly Father loves to reveal His secrets of love. Amen.

Our Father, Hail Mary, Glory be to the Father.

4th Prayer

O Jesus, my Savior, be mindful of the profound sadness that You felt when Your enemies surrounded You and tormented You in a thousand ways. They attacked You, spit in Your glorious face, struck You, and even slapped You, saying: "Prophesy for us, Messiah: who is it that struck You?" (Mt 26:68).

Led before the Sanhedrin, You endured in silence the accusations of numerous false witnesses. Then, brought before Herod, You were treated like an imposter magician and a fool. You were returned to Pilate derisively clothed in a robe of royal purple.

In consideration of these torments that You endured with great patience, I beg You, my Savior, to deliver us from all our visible and invisible enemies so that through Your grace we may attain eternal salvation. Amen.

Our Father, Hail Mary, Glory be to the Father.

5th Prayer

Praised be You, O Jesus, my Lord, for letting Yourself be bound to the pillar where You were atrociously scourged, after which You were manifested all bloody at the tribunal of Pilate as the innocent Lamb, standing and already immolated (see Rv 5:6).

In consideration of Your infinite patience, I beg You, my Savior, to strengthen our own patience in the trials of life, especially those that come to us from the hands of unjust and cruel persons. Grant this grace to us and conversion to them. Amen.

Our Father, Hail Mary, Glory be to the Father.

6th Prayer

Praised be You, O Jesus, my Lord, for having willed to be condemned to death like a criminal to bring about our salvation. You painfully carried Your Cross to the place of Your Passion. After Your executioners removed Your garments, they immobilized Your members, pierced them with large nails, and affixed You to the Cross by painfully stretching out Your aching Body.

In consideration of these torments, I beg You, my Savior, to grant us a hatred for sin and a love for what is pleasing to You. Amen.

Our Father, Hail Mary, Glory be to the Father.

7th Prayer

Eternal glory to You, O Jesus, my Savior, for from the gibbet of the Cross, naked and miserable, You saw Yourself abandoned by all Your relatives, disciples, and friends, with no one near You except for a few faithful souls. In the midst of an ocean of sufferings, You did not cease to pray. You interceded for Your enemies by saying: "Father, forgive them, they know not what they do" (Lk 23:34).

Gazing lovingly on Your noble Mother who had never sinned, You consoled her by entrusting to her Your beloved disciple with these words: "Woman, behold your son." Then turning to John, You said to him: "Behold, your mother" (Jn 19:26-27).

In consideration of this great mercy that You showed for us even to the Cross, I beg You, my Savior, to impress in our souls the remembrance of Your Passion, perfect repentance for our sins, and a greater under-standing of Your Love for us. Amen.

Our Father, Hail Mary, Glory be to the Father.

8th Prayer

Praised be You eternally, O Jesus, my Lord, for in the torments of Your last agony You willed to give all sinners the hope of pardon by promising the glory of paradise to the thief who turned to You. You reassured him with these words: "Today you will be with me in Paradise" (Lk 23:43).

Through this abyss of compassion for sinful souls, I beg You, my Savior, to show us a similar mercy at the hour of our death. Amen.

Our Father, Hail Mary, Glory be to the Father.

9th Prayer

Eternal praise be Yours, O Jesus, my Lord, for those long hours during which on the Cross You endured for us the greatest pains and the most extreme anguish. The acute sufferings from Your wounds also pierced Your most holy soul. In Your humanity, which bore all the weight of the sin of the world, You felt like one rejected by Your Father.

When all the prophecies of suffering were finally accomplished in You, You could cry out: "It is finished" (Jn 19:30). Then, before letting Your Heart break under the impulsion of Your Divine Love, You directed Your last prayer toward heaven: "Father, into your hands I commend my spirit" (Lk 23:46). Then bowing Your head, You humbly entrusted Your spirit into the hands of God the Father.

In consideration of Your death out of love, which abolished Satan's domination of our wounded race, I beg You, my Savior, to grant us the immense grace of dying like You. May we die with sentiments of love and confidence toward the Father, totally united with You and Your blessed Mother and free from all attachment to sin. Amen.

Our Father, Hail Mary, Glory be to the Father.

10th Prayer

Praised be You, O Jesus, my Lord, for redeeming our souls by Your precious Blood and Your holy Death. You descended to the kingdom of the dead to seek out all the just souls who were awaiting You from the time of Adam, and You mercifully led them out of exile to eternal life.

In consideration for the fulfillment of the Biblical promises concerning the entry of the just into paradise, I beg You, my Savior, to convert us totally and enduringly, so that we can all come to join You in heaven where You have already prepared a place for us in the company of Your Mother, the Angels, and the Saints. Amen.

Our Father, Hail Mary, Glory be to the Father.

11th Prayer

Praised be You, O Jesus, my Lord, for in order to better manifest Your Love to us You allowed Your Heart to be pierced by a lance, thus liberating a precious stream of Blood and water, symbols of the Eucharist and Baptism.

Since You had already expired, this blow was sorrowfully felt by Your Mother who, at the foot of the Cross, continued to pray.

In consideration of Mary's motherly sorrow and of Your Heart opened for us as a Source of purification and holiness, I beg You, my Savior, to strengthen our faith in Your Sacraments of salvation, especially the Eucharist in which You actualize for us Your redemptive offering of the Last Supper and Calvary. Amen.

Our Father, Hail Mary, Glory be to the Father.

12th Prayer

Praised be You, O Jesus, my Lord, because You willed that Your most holy Body should be taken down from the Cross by Your friends Joseph and Nicodemus and given into the care of Your afflicted Mother. Your Body was thus washed, wrapped with cloths, placed in the tomb, and finally guarded by soldiers.

In consideration of the sentiments of infinite distress felt by Your Mother and Your friends as they accompanied Your broken Body to the tomb, I beg You, my Savior, to have mercy on those who die alone and have no one to weep and pray for them. Amen.

Our Father, Hail Mary, Glory be to the Father.

13th Prayer

Glory to You, O Jesus, my Lord, for on the morning of the third day You rose from the dead and manifested Yourself to witnesses of Your choice.

Glory again to You, for after forty days You ascended to heaven in the sight of a vast number of Your disciples and there crowned the just whom You had delivered from the netherworld.

In consideration of these glorious events, I beg You, my Savior, to strengthen our hope in the fulfillment of all Your promises concerning our eternal life. Amen.

Our Father, Hail Mary, Glory be to the Father.

14th Prayer

Eternal joy and praise to You, O Jesus, my Lord, for according to Your promise You sent the Holy Spirit into the hearts of Your faithful where He stirred up a very great love for God and neighbor.

In consideration of this pouring out of Your Love upon the first disciples, I beg You, my Savior, to grant also to us, according to our needs, the effusion of Your Spirit, so that we may be more and more inflamed with the supernatural Fire that makes Saints. Amen.

Our Father, Hail Mary, Glory be to the Father.

15th Prayer

Eternally blessed, praised, and glorified may You be, O Jesus, my Lord, for You are enthroned in Your Kingdom of Heaven in the glory of Your Divinity, living in a resurrected way with the most holy Body that was formed in the womb of the Immaculate Virgin. And it is in this glory that You will come on the last day to judge the living and the dead.

In consideration of these holy mysteries of salvation that we have meditated upon in the presence of Your Son, O Father most holy, grant us the grace to share one day the eternal Joy of the children of God! Amen.

Our Father, Hail Mary, Glory be to the Father.

PRAYER IN TIME OF GRAVE SICKNESS

Lord Jesus, I am gravely ill, I feel threatened, and I find no comfort around me. You Who are always present, hear my cries and transform them into prayers! I offer to You all these painful moments as so many acts of love.

Nevertheless, please assuage my physical and moral sufferings! You Who can do all things, come quickly to comfort me! Send at least Your Angel of Consolation to give me peace! Send me at least Your Mother to help me carry this cross that is also Your own, O my Crucified Savior! Amen.

—Father Bernard-Marie

LITANY OF THE HOLY PASSION OF CHRIST

The invocations of this beautiful Litany are unfortunately little known in our day. Formerly, they were more particularly recited in cases of serious illness or in time of a great trial (mourning, war, epidemic, or natural cataclysm). Even today, they could still be a source of grace and comfort for us.

Lord, have mercy.
Christ, have mercy.
Lord, have mercy.
Christ, hear us.
Christ, graciously hear us.
God the Father of heaven, *have mercy on us.*
God the Son, Redeemer of the world, *have mercy on us.*
God the Holy Spirit, *have mercy on us.*
Holy Trinity, one God, *have mercy on us.*

O Mary, coredemptrix and mediatrix, *pray for us.*

Jesus, King of glory making Your entry into Jerusalem to complete the work of our redemption, *have mercy on us.**

Jesus, prostrate before Your Father in the Garden of Olives and burdened with the crimes of the whole world,

---

*Have mercy on us is said after each invocation.

Jesus, gripped with fear, overcome with sadness, reduced to an agony, covered with a bloody sweat, and abandoned by all,

Jesus, betrayed by one of those closest to You and sold at a vile price as a slave,

Jesus, bound, struck, dishonored, dragged to Annas and Caiaphas, treated like an irreligious blasphemer,

Jesus, brought before Pilate and accused of being an agitator and a dangerous rebel,

Jesus, appearing before Herod, treated like a fool and clothed in a robe of royal purple,

Jesus, cruelly struck with 39 lashes of the triple thonged Roman whip covered with lead that tore Your Body in more than 120 spots,

Jesus, crowned with thorns, arrayed in a robe of purple, dishonored and ridiculed in various ways, then exposed to the eyes of all,

Jesus, likened to a seditious criminal who was preferred to You,

Jesus, cowardly condemned by Pilate and abandoned to the rage of Your enemies,

Jesus, exhausted by sufferings and trudging toward Calvary under the burden of Your Cross,

Jesus, stripped of Your garments, placed on the ground, and violently stretched out on the wood of the Cross,

Jesus, nailed without pity to the wood of infamy and placed in the ranks of the greatest sinners,

Jesus, full of kindness toward those who offered You a drink of wine mixed with myrrh,

Jesus, praying to Your Father and asking grace for Your persecutors and executioners,

Jesus, showing Yourself obedient to Your Father even to death and commending Your spirit into His hands,

Jesus, bowing Your head and giving up Your spirit out of the ardor of Your love for us,

Jesus, dead for us and letting Your Heart be opened by the thrust of a lance in order to better manifest to us Your mercy that is forever offered,

Lamb of God, You take away the sins of the world; *spare us, O Lord.*

Lamb of God, You take away the sins of the world; *graciously hear us, O Lord.*

Lamb of God, You take away the sins of the world; *have mercy on us, O Lord.*

Let us pray. O Jesus, You have redeemed us by dying out of love on the Cross. Apply to us the merits of Your holy Passion and Death and grant that by these merits we may obtain the signal grace that we ask of Your mercy *(mention it here)*. We earnestly beg You to take into account also the prayers and sufferings of Your holy Mother at the foot of the Cross. ℟. *Amen.*

WAY OF THE CROSS

Although the prayers given above can often take the place of making the Stations of the Cross, it would be preferable to practice this devotion especially on Fridays. Numerous graces can be obtained by the practice of this "mini-pilgrimage" to the Holy Land with Christ.

Opening Prayer

Heavenly Father, grant that we who meditate on the Passion and Death of Your Son, Jesus Christ, may imitate in our lives His love and self-giving to You and to others. We ask this through Christ our Lord.

1. Jesus Is Condemned to Death

"God so loved the world that he gave his only Son, so that . . . the world might be saved through him" (Jn 3:16-17).

Let us pray. Father, in the flesh of Your Son You condemned sin. Grant us the gift of eternal life in the same Christ our Lord.

2. Jesus Bears His Cross

"If anyone wishes to come after me, he must deny himself and take up his cross daily and follow me" (Lk 9:23).

Let us pray. Father, Your Son Jesus humbled Himself and became obedient to death. Teach us to glory above all else in the Cross, in which is our salvation. Grant this through Christ our Lord.

3. Jesus Falls the First Time

"The Lord laid upon him the guilt of us all" (Is 53:6). "Behold, the Lamb of God, who takes away the sin of the world" (Jn 1:29).

Let us pray. Father, help us to remain irreproachable in Your sight, so that we can offer You our body as a holy and living offering. We ask this in the name of Jesus the Lord.

4. Jesus Meets His Holy Mother

"Come, all you who pass by the way, look and see whether there is any suffering like my suffering" (Lam 1:12).

Let us pray. Father, accept the sorrows of the Blessed Virgin Mary, Mother of Your Son. May they obtain from Your mercy every good for our salvation. Grant this through Christ our Lord.

5. Jesus Is Helped by Simon

"Whatever you did for one of these least brothers of mine, you did for me" (Mt 25:40).

Let us pray. Father, You have first loved us and You sent Your Son to expiate our sins. Grant that we may love one another and bear each other's burdens. We ask this through Christ our Lord.

6. Veronica Wipes the Face of Jesus

"His look was marred beyond that of man, and his appearance beyond that of mortals" (Is 52:14). "Whoever has seen me has seen the Father" (Jn 14:9).

Let us pray. Heavenly Father, grant that we may reflect Your Son's glory and be transformed into His image so that we may be configured to Him. We ask this in the name of Jesus.

7. Jesus Falls a Second Time

"We do not have a high priest who is unable to sympathize with our weaknesses, but one who has similarly been tested in every way, yet without sin" (Heb 4:15).

Let us pray. God our Father, grant that we may walk in the footsteps of Jesus, Who suffered for us and redeemed us not with gold and silver but with the price of His own Blood. We ask this through Christ our Lord.

8. Jesus Speaks to the Women

"Daughters of Jerusalem, do not weep for me; weep instead for yourselves and for your children" (Lk 23:28).

Let us pray. Heavenly Father, You desire to show mercy rather than anger toward all who hope in You. Grant that we may weep for our sins and merit the grace of Your glory. We ask this in the name of Jesus the Lord.

9. Jesus Falls a Third Time

"Have among yourselves the same attitude that is also yours in Christ Jesus, who . . . emptied himself, taking the form of a slave" (Phil 2:5-7).

Let us pray. God our Father, look with pity on us oppressed by the weight of our sins and grant us Your forgiveness. Help us to serve You with our whole heart. We ask this through Christ our Lord.

10. Jesus Is Stripped of His Garments

"They divide my garments among them, and for my vesture they cast lots" (Ps 22:19).

Let us pray. Heavenly Father, let nothing deprive us of Your love—neither trials nor distress nor persecution. May we become the wheat of Christ and be one pure bread. Grant this through Christ our Lord.

11. Jesus Is Nailed to the Cross

"They have pierced my hands and my feet; I can count all my bones" (Ps 22:17f).

Let us pray. Heavenly Father, Your Son reconciled us to You and to one another. Help us to embrace His gift of grace and remain united with You. We ask this through Christ our Lord.

12. Jesus Dies on the Cross

"When I am lifted up from the earth, I will draw everyone to myself" (Jn 12:32).

Let us pray. God our Father, by His Death Your Son has conquered death, and by His Resurrection He has given us life. Help us to adore His Death and embrace His Life. Grant this in the name of Jesus the Lord.

13. Jesus Is Taken Down
from the Cross

"Was it not necessary that the Messiah should suffer these things and enter into his glory?" (Lk 24:26).

Let us pray. God our Father, grant that we may be associated in Christ's Death so that we may advance toward the resurrection with great hope. We ask this through Christ our Lord.

14. Jesus Is Placed in the Tomb

"Unless a grain of wheat falls to the ground and dies, it remains just a grain of wheat; but if it dies, it produces much fruit" (Jn 12:24). "Christ . . . was raised on the third day in accordance with the scriptures" (1 Cor 15:3-4).

Let us pray. Heavenly Father, You raised Jesus from the dead through Your Holy Spirit. Grant life to our mortal bodies through that same Spirit Who abides in us. We ask this in the name of Jesus the Lord.

Concluding Prayer

Heavenly Father, You delivered Your Son to the death of the Cross to save us from evil. Grant us the grace of the resurrection. We ask this through Christ our Lord.

GOD THE HOLY SPIRIT: OUR SANCTIFIER
AND GUIDE — The Holy Spirit guides us in the
way of sanctification and salvation. As he
descended on Jesus at His baptism by John, so
He descends on us at Baptism and inspires us
to a loving union with God through actions and
prayer.

4. PRAYERS TO THE HOLY SPIRIT

No grace, no miracle, no Sacrament comes to us without the Holy Spirit playing an integral role in it. It is the Spirit Who raised Jesus (Rom 8:11) and filled the disciples with extraordinary gifts (1 Cor 12:10). And it is the Spirit for Whom we ask in our most "inspired" prayers even when we think we are praying only for a very human intention.

Since it is the Spirit of the Father and of the Son Who comes to act in the multiple responses to our prayers, we should from time to time speak to Him face to face, open ourselves to His Love, and thank Him in advance for all His gifts.

PRAYER FOR CONSOLATION

Comforting Lord, gift from on high,
Seeking Your aid, we send our cry!
Fount of all life! Fire of God's love!
Be our anointing from above.

Holy Spirit, Divine Comforter,
comfort me in all my sorrows!

PRAYER FOR THE INDWELLING
OF THE SPIRIT

Holy Spirit, powerful Consoler, sacred Bond of the Father and the Son, Hope of the afflicted, descend into my heart and establish in it Your loving dominion. Enkindle in my tepid soul the fire of Your love so that I may be wholly subject to You.

We believe that when You dwell in us, You also prepare a dwelling for the Father and the Son. Deign, therefore, to come to me, Consoler of abandoned souls and Protector of the needy. Help the afflicted, strengthen the weak, and support the wavering.

Come and purify me. Let no evil desire take possession of me. You love the humble and resist the proud. Come to me, Glory of the living and Hope of the dying. Lead me by Your grace that I may always be pleasing to You.

St. Augustine of Hippo

LITANY OF THE HOLY SPIRIT

God the Father of heaven, *have mercy on us.*

God the Son, Redeemer of the world, *have mercy on us.*

God the Holy Spirit, *have mercy on us.*

Holy Spirit, Who proceed from the Father and the Son, *come to dwell in us.**

Spirit of the Lord, Who fill the whole universe,

Holy Spirit, of Whom Jesus was conceived in the womb of the Virgin Mary,

Spirit of wisdom and understanding,

Spirit of counsel and fortitude,

Spirit of knowledge and piety,

Spirit of fear of the Lord,

Spirit of faith, hope, and love,

Spirit of humility and mercy,

Spirit of justice and holiness,

Spirit of truth,

Holy Spirit, comforter,

Holy Spirit, Who pour forth love into our hearts,

Holy Spirit, Who descended on the Apostles,

Holy Spirit, Who inspire us to do good,

Holy Spirit, Who move us to practice true prayer,

Holy Spirit, Who keep us from evil,

Holy Spirit, Who protect us from the devil,

Holy Spirit, Who deliver us from temptations,

---

* *Come to dwell in us* is recited after each invocation.

Holy Spirit, Who fill us with joy,

Holy Spirit, Who make us pure,

Holy Spirit, Who make us Your temple,

Holy Spirit, Whom we can sadden,

Holy Spirit, Who render us attentive to the inspirations of the Angels,

Holy Spirit, Who inspire peace and love,

Holy Spirit, Who are our only strength,

Holy Spirit, gift of the Father and the Son,

Holy Spirit, Whom we adore,

℣. Lord, send forth Your Spirit.

℟. *And He will renew the face of the earth!*

Let us pray. Father most gracious, through Jesus You have promised that whoever asks for Your Holy Spirit with the trust of a child will not be disappointed (Lk 11:13). With faith in this word, we dare already to thank You for the sacred Gift that You wish to make to us. In union with this Divine Spirit, we wish to offer You the world and our lives as Your Son Jesus did on the Cross of salvation. ℟. *Amen.*

PRAYER TO RECEIVE THE HOLY SPIRIT

HOLY Spirit, Lord of Light,

from Your clear celestial height,

Your pure beaming radiance give.

Come, O Father of the Poor,
come with treasures that endure,
come, O Light of all that live.

You of all Consolers best,
and the soul's delightsome Guest,
do refreshing Peace bestow.

You in toil are Comfort sweet,
pleasant Coolness in the heat,
solace in the midst of woe.

Light immortal, Light Divine,
visit now this heart of mine,
and my inmost being fill.

If You take Your grace away,
nothing pure in us will stay,
all our good is turned to ill.

Heal our wounds, our strength renew,
on our dryness pour your Dew,
wash the stains of guilt away.

Bend the stubborn heart and will,
melt the frozen, warm the chill,
guide the steps that go astray.

On all those who evermore
You confess and You adore,
in Your *Sevenfold Gifts* descend.

Give them *Comfort* when they die.
Give them Life with You on high,
give them Joys that never end.

MARY: MOTHER, QUEEN, AND MEDIATRIX
— Of all the Saints, Mary the Mother of Our
Lord is by far the favorite of all Christians. She
has been invoked throughout the centuries by
all classes of Christians for all types of requests, and her clients have invariably been
heard. Her intercession with her Son began at
the Marriage Feast of Cana and continues to
this day from her heavenly seat.

5. PRAYERS TO OUR LADY

THE HAIL MARY

Hail Mary, full of grace,
the Lord is with you.
Blessed are you among women
and blessed is the fruit of your womb,
  Jesus.
Holy Mary, Mother of God,
pray for us sinners,
now and at the hour of our death. Amen.

THE ROSARY

Let us recall that the Rosary consists in the recitation of three chaplets with the meditation of the three great series of mysteries of the Life of Christ: the joyful, sorrowful, and glorious mysteries.

Thanks to numerous great Saints, we know that the Blessed Virgin can obtain special graces for us to be heard and assisted if we but greet her often with this means that she loves so much: the meditated Rosary.*

It is this conviction that led St. Vincent de Paul to say: "After the Mass, the Rosary makes more

*To know and pray the Rosary better, you might consult the booklet *Praying the Rosary* and the book *The Mystery of the Rosary* by Father Marc Tremeau—both published by Catholic Book Publishing Co.

graces descend into souls than any other prayer."
Or again, Pope Leo XIII: "There are numerous
means of obtaining Mary's assistance. However,
we believe that the institution of the Rosary is the
best *and most fruitful."*

HOW TO SAY THE ROSARY

1. *Begin on the crucifix and say the Apostles' Creed.*
2. *On the 1st bead, say 1 Our Father.*
3. *On the next 3 beads, say Hail Mary.*
4. *Next say 1 Glory Be. Then announce and think of the first Mystery and say 1 Our Father.*
5. *Say 10 Hail Marys and 1 Glory be to the Father.*
6. *Announce the second Mystery and continue in the same way until each of the five Mysteries of the selected group of decades is said.*

The Joyful Mysteries

1. **The Angel Gabriel brings the joyful message to Mary (Lk 1:26-38).**
2. **Mary visits her cousin Elizabeth (Lk 1:41-50).**
3. **Jesus is born in a stable in Bethlehem (Lk 2:1-14).**
4. **Jesus is offered in the Temple (Lk 2:22-40).**
5. **Jesus is found again in the Temple (Lk 2:42-52).**

The Sorrowful Mysteries

1. **Jesus prays in agony to His Heavenly Father (Mt 26:36-40).**
2. **Jesus is scourged (Mt 27:42-46).**
3. **Jesus is crowned with thorns (Mt 26:27-31).**
4. **Jesus carries His Cross to Calvary (Mt 27:32).**
5. **Jesus dies on the Cross (Mt 27:33-50).**

The Glorious Mysteries

1. **Jesus rises from death (Mk 16:1-7).**
2. **Jesus ascends to heaven (Mk 16:14-20).**
3. **The Holy Spirit descends upon the Apostles (Acts 2:1-11).**
4. **Mary is taken up to heaven in body and soul (Lk 1:41-50).**
5. **Mary is crowned in heaven (Rv 12:1).**

THE "HAIL, HOLY QUEEN"

This prayer nicely expresses the sometimes difficult and painful aspect of our human condition. We could pray it as an introduction to another prayer to Our Lady.

Hail, holy Queen, Mother of mercy;
hail, our life, our sweetness, and our hope.
To you do we cry,
poor banished children of Eve.
To you do we send up our sighs,
mourning and weeping in this valley of
   tears.
Turn then, most gracious Advocate,
your eyes of mercy toward us.
And after this our exile
show unto us the blessed fruit of your
   womb, Jesus.
O clement, O loving, O sweet Virgin Mary.

THE "MEMORARE"

This prayer of filial insistence and unwavering hope could serve as a frequent conclusion for our other prayers and devotions to Our Lady.

Remember, O most gracious Virgin Mary,
that never was it known
that anyone who fled to your protection,
implored your help or sought your interces-
    sion
was left unaided.
Inspired with this confidence,
I fly to you, O Virgin of virgins, my
    Mother;
to you do I come,
before you I stand, sinful and sorrowful.
O Mother of the Word Incarnate,
despise not my petitions,
but in your mercy hear and answer me.
Amen.

THE "SUB TUUM"
AN ANCIENT MARIAN PRAYER

We fly to your patronage,
O holy Mother of God;
despise not our petitions in our necessities,
but deliver us always from all dangers,
O glorious and blessed Virgin.

PRAYER OF ABBÉ PERREYVE

O Holy Virgin, in the midst of your days of glory, do not forget the sorrows of earth. Cast a kindly look on those who are suffering, those who struggle against difficulties and keep a stiff upper lip in all life's afflictions.

Have mercy on those who love one another and have been separated.

Have mercy on those who suffer from isolation of the heart.

Have mercy on the weakness of our faith.

Have mercy on those we love.

Have mercy on those who pray, those who tremble, and those who weep.

Give to all the hope of peace! Amen.

INVOCATIONS TO THE IMMACULATE HEART OF MARY

On June 13, 1917, the Blessed Virgin spoke in these words to the little visionary Lucy of Fatima: "Jesus desires to establish in the world the devotion to my Immaculate Heart. I promise salvation to anyone who shall adopt this devotion, and the souls that practice it will be dear to God. They will be like flowers placed by me to adorn His throne." These solemn promises are in perfect accord with those that the Blessed Virgin addressed 87 years previously to St. Catherine Labouré in the chapel of the Rue de Bac in Paris (they are cited above on p. 14).

The Church herself has recommended invoking Mary often with this appellation of Immaculate. Therefore, there is every reason to believe that if it is done with filial love it will be pleasing to God and draw down upon us all kinds of blessings. We propose the following invocations because they are short and especially adapted to the context of urgent occasions and causes.

Sorrowful and Immaculate Heart of Mary, pray for us.

Sorrowful and Immaculate Heart of Mary, intercede for us.

Sorrowful and Immaculate Heart of Mary, help us.

Sorrowful and Immaculate Heart of Mary, comfort us.

Sorrowful and Immaculate Heart of Mary, protect us.

LITANY OF THE BLESSED VIRGIN MARY

It is the constant teaching of Scripture that if brief prayers are generally those most appreciated by God, it in no way displeases Him if we repeat them with a certain insistence: "He told them a parable about the necessity for them to pray always without becoming weary" (Lk 18:1); "Pray at every opportunity . . . with all perseverance" (Eph 6:18).

The reason for these repetitions is obviously not that God is deaf or slow to understand but that in His infinite goodness He has willed to grant us certain choice graces after we have only manifested a minimum of love and persevering effort. In this respect St. Augustine reminds us that although long discourses have not been required of us, "a long discourse is one thing but quite another is a long love!"

It is thus in this confident and persevering spirit of love that we are now invited to pray to the Blessed Virgin Mary with the following Litany. We have retouched it lightly in order to insert in it the new titles given Mary by the Second Vatican Council.

Lord, have mercy.
Christ, have mercy.
Lord, have mercy.

Holy Mary, pray for us.
Holy Mother of God, pray for us.
Holy Virgin of virgins, pray for us.
Mother of Jesus, pray for us.
Mother of the Messiah, pray for us.

Mother of the Savior, pray for us.
Mother of the Lord, pray for us.
Mother conceived without sin, pray for us.
Mother most pure, pray for us.
Mother most chaste, pray for us.
Mother inviolate, pray for us.
Mother ever virgin, pray for us.
Mother most amiable, pray for us.
Mother most admirable, pray for us.
Mother of true love, pray for us.
Mother of mercy, pray for us.
Mother of hope, pray for us.
Mother of the Church, pray for us.
Mother of all human beings, pray for us.
Mother blessed among mothers, pray for us.

Virgin filled with grace, pray for us.
Virgin most holy, pray for us.
Virgin most humble, pray for us.
Virgin most poor, pray for us.
Virgin most believing, pray for us.
Virgin most obedient, pray for us.
Virgin most prayerful, pray for us.
Virgin most prudent, pray for us.
Virgin most faithful, pray for us.
Virgin full of suffering, pray for us.
Virgin full of joy, pray for us.
Virgin full of goodness, pray for us.

Virgin most powerful, pray for us.
Virgin blessed among virgins, pray for us.

New Eve, pray for us.
Daughter of Zion, pray for us.
Heir of the promise, pray for us.
Servant of the Lord, pray for us.
Ark of the Covenant, pray for us.
City of God, pray for us.
Seat of wisdom, pray for us.
Temple of the Holy Spirit, pray for us.
House filled with glory, pray for us.
House of gold, pray for us.
Mystical rose, pray for us.
Tower of David, pray for us.
Tower of ivory, pray for us.
Morning star, pray for us.
Gate of heaven, pray for us.
Splendor of the world, pray for us.
Woman blessed among women, pray for us.

Mediatrix of grace, pray for us.
Dispensatrix of grace, pray for us.
Strength of the consecrated, pray for us.
Model of spouses, pray for us.
Help of Christians, pray for us.
Comforter of the afflicted, pray for us.
Advocate of the oppressed, pray for us.
Health of the sick, pray for us.

Refuge of sinners, pray for us.
Cause of our joy, pray for us.

Our Lady of Perpetual Help, pray for us.
Our Lady of Sorrows, pray for us.
Our Lady of Lourdes, pray for us.
Our Lady of Mount Carmel, pray for us.
Our Lady of the Rosary, pray for us.
Our Lady of Peace, pray for us.

Queen assumed into heaven, pray for us.
Queen of angels, pray for us.
Queen of archangels, pray for us.
Queen of patriarchs, pray for us.
Queen of prophets, pray for us.
Queen of apostles, pray for us.
Queen of martyrs, pray for us.
Queen of confessors, pray for us.
Queen of pastors, pray for us.
Queen of missionaries, pray for us.
Queen of doctors, pray for us.
Queen of virgins, pray for us.
Queen of consecrated souls, pray for us.
Queen of the faithful, pray for us.
Queen of the poor, pray for us.
Queen of the afflicted, pray for us.
Queen of all saints, pray for us.
Queen of the world to come, pray for us.

Lamb of God, You take away the sins of
the world; spare us, O Lord!

Lamb of God, You take away the sins of
the world; graciously hear us, O Lord.
Lamb of God, You take away the sins of
the world; have mercy on us.

Let us pray. Lord Jesus, we have just
meditated on the wonders with which You
enriched Mary, Your Mother, whom You
have given to us. Now, through her intercession, grant that we may live in greater
fidelity to Your Holy Spirit and one day attain eternal bliss with You in the company
of Mary and Your Church. ℞. *Amen.*

NOVENA TO OUR LADY OF PERPETUAL HELP

*Here is one of the most popular novenas dedi-
cated to Our Lady. Leading us to meditate on the
Sorrows of the Mother of Christ at the moment of
His Passion, it is in some way the Marian equiva-
lent of the Fifteen Prayers of St. Bridget (see p.
46).*

*This novena is prayed for nine successive days, if
possible before an image of Our Lady of Perpetual
Help. A reproduction will be found on the front
cover of this book. It is inspired directly by a
Byzantine icon of the Cretan painter Andreas
Ritzos (end of the 15th century). Numerous copies*

and variants of it exist throughout the world. This universal popularity is doubtless explained by the fact that countless unexpected favors have been obtained by a fervent prayer recited at the foot of this celebrated "Virgin of the Passion."

1st Day

O Mother of Perpetual Help, I love to come to pray at the foot of your wondrous image! It inspires in me sentiments of the most lively and most filial trust. You hold in your arms Jesus, my Savior and my God. He is the All-Powerful One, the absolute Master of life and death, the sovereign Dispenser of all good and all grace. And you are His Mother!

Therefore, you have every right to pray to Him and every right to be heard. Moreover, He has often proven—to us poor sinners—that He cannot and will not refuse you anything.

Hence, I address your all-powerful intercession, O Mother of Jesus, and I beg you to grant me during this novena the grace . . . (*here indicate the intention for this novena*).

I come to ask your intercession with complete confidence, because I am convinced that you never cease to pray for your children, and thus also for me.

Add an Our Father (p. 33), a Hail Mary (p. 77), and a Memorare (p. 80).

2nd Day

O Mother of Perpetual Help, in this Child Jesus still so feeble Whom you press to your heart, you see more than the Son of God and your Son. You see also all human beings—who have become your children through the will of God and through your self-giving at Nazareth and on Calvary. You never forget the word of your Son on Calvary Who, considering His disciple John and all of us in him, said to you: "Behold, your son" (John 19:26).

O Mother, with the directness of an unhappy child, I come to tell you how I suffer and am tempted to despair. However, I know that I am your child and that you hear all our prayers. O Mother, you know my request: please answer it for the greater glory of your Son, my Savior!

Our Father, Hail Mary, Memorare.

3rd Day

O Mother of Perpetual Help, I love to contemplate your blessed image. It speaks to me with eloquence about all your greatness. On your right I see Gabriel the Archangel, the Divine Ambassador who greeted you with the absolutely unique title of "Full of grace." On the left I see Michael the Archangel whose presence reminds us that you command all the heavenly hosts. In your right hand you hold the hands of the King of kings.

All this reminds me that you are the Woman blessed among all women, the most beautiful ornament of the universe, the creature alone judged worthy to become the Mother of the Word Incarnate. You are the Immaculata, the All-Holy, the masterpiece of the Most High. You are the Queen of heaven and earth, the great honor of our humanity.

O Mother most admirable, instead of frightening me, your incomparable greatness only increases my confidence. If God, in His goodness, has made you so holy and so powerful, it is for our salvation, and if you rejoice over your privileges, it is because they better enable you to help us.

O Mother without compare, grant me the grace that I ask of your maternal tenderness.

Our Father, Hail Mary, Memorare.

4th Day

O Mother of Perpetual Help, your maternal gaze comforts our anxious and wounded hearts. You appear to us like the sacred Stem that gives rise to the Flower of all purity and all virtue, your Jesus, our God. As we offer Him through your maternal hands, our hearts are opened more widely to His coming and to His plans for us.

On your forehead there shines a radiant star. Indeed, are you not the "Morning Star" who announce the day of salvation and redemption? Are you not the one who recalls to us the Gospel promise of the day without end and a blessed eternity? Are you not also the "Star of the Sea" who radiates hope amidst the blackest of storms?

O Mother most amiable, how light you render for us the burden of duty and how sweet the yoke of Jesus Christ! The re-

membrance of you puts joy in my heart and
the invocation of your name restores peace
to my troubled soul. Let me always repeat
before you: O Mother so worthy of love, I
love you! Through you and with you, I love
your Divine Son! O holy Mother of hope,
hear me!

Our Father, Hail Mary, Memorare.

5th Day

O Mother of Perpetual Help, I find in your
holy image another reason to hope in your
goodness. You always show yourself
therein as the Mother of sorrows. The One
whom you hold tight in your arms is Jesus,
crucified in His heart before being crucified
in His flesh. Already the instruments of the
Passion are represented to Him and you
suffer with Him at this prophetic sight.

Like you, O Mary, I compassionate with
the sufferings of your Son and, like Him, I
compassionate with your own sufferings.
My compassion is all the more ardent as it
is our sins that by nailing Jesus to the Cross
have tormented your most loving soul.
Today, it is in the name of your sorrows
that I pray. Grant me contrition for all my

sins and the courage to avoid them in the future. And be pleased to favor the request that I address to you in this novena.

Our Father, Hail Mary, Memorare.

6th Day

O Mother of Perpetual Help, because you are good and are also our Mother, suffering has led you to have compassion on our pains. I see this compassion toward us in your eyes shining with tender pity. They are fixed less on your Divine Son than on your poor children on earth. How sweet it is for a crushed soul to encounter a friendly heart that knows how to be compassionate! And when that heart is the heart of a mother, and of a mother such as you, it is one of the greatest consolations in life.

Therefore, I come at your feet to regain my courage, O compassionate Mother! I am sure that you will not abandon your child. Hear the cry of my wretchedness. Speak the word of consolation to my soul and grant me the favor that I ask of your goodness.

Our Father, Hail Mary, Memorare.

7th Day

O Mother of Perpetual Help, you are the Mediatrix of all grace. Yes, you are the treasury of our God Who desires that all grace should pass through your hands before it is given to us. Your image reminds me that you are the Mother of Jesus, the Mother of sorrows, and my Mother also.

As the Mother of Jesus, you are most closely united with the Heart of your Son. As the Mother of sorrows, you united your sufferings with those of Jesus and cooperated in our salvation. As the Mother of human beings, you accepted to come to our aid.

Yes, I know, a soul faithful in invoking you is sure of your protection and a soul protected by you cannot be lost. It is thus with assurance that I have recourse to you. Obtain for me, after your example, fidelity in the service of the things of God. And also obtain for me the favor that during this novena I request from your maternal tenderness.

Our Father, Hail Mary, Memorare.

8th Day

O Mother of Perpetual Help, sometimes a feeling of fear grips my heart. Indeed, when I think of how wretched I am, I find it audacious on my part to dare to address you and ask for your favors. However, your sweet image seems to say to me: "Confidence, my child! Am I not the Mother of mercy who seek not merits to reward but evils to heal? Does not my title of Mother of Perpetual Help proclaim that God sends me to you to relieve you in His Name of all your miseries?"

It is thus to your clemency that I appeal today, O Mary. My confidence rests entirely on your indulgent and compassionate goodness. It is for you to protect me, to help me, and to console me in the best way you know.

Our Father, Hail Mary, Memorare.

9th Day

O Mother of Perpetual Help, I have reached the end of this novena, wherein each day I have come to kneel at your feet. Today, more than ever, my supplication rises ardently and confidently to you. I have no doubt that you have heard the cry of my prayer and will grant what I ask or an even more precious grace. Through your Son crucified for us, through your sorrows united with His, through your merciful love, through your title as Mother of Perpetual Help, grant my petition if such is the will of God!

Dear Mother, my confidence is so great that from this moment I will say thank you! Thank you for the past graces; thank you for those that I await from your inexhaustible love. O Mother of Consolation, as Jesus gave you to us, now give us Jesus forever, for He is the Grace of graces! Amen.

Our Father, Hail Mary, Memorare.

LITANY OF OUR LADY OF LOURDES

The Marian appearances at Lourdes resemble those at the Rue du Bac and at Fatima because of the place that Mary's first great privilege—her conception without sin—*has in them. This privilege enabled Mary to maintain an Adam-like freedom that she fully utilized for God at the moment of her "fiat" ("Let it be done") at the Annunciation. In the light of the importance of this Marian privilege in the process that would lead to our salvation in Jesus Christ, it may be useful to give several points of historical information on this subject.*

It was on December 8, 1854, that Pope Pius IX solemnly proclaimed the dogma of Mary's Immaculate Conception. From that date on, the Church universally and officially confesses that the Mother of the Redeemer, "in view of the merits of Jesus Christ," was miraculously preserved from her conception from all original stain and inclination to evil.

Less than four years later, on March 25, 1858, the Blessed Virgin Mary appeared to the humble Bernadette of Lourdes and said to her: "I am the Immaculate Conception."

Since the last of her 18 appearances on July 16, 1858, the Blessed Virgin has not ceased to obtain for pilgrims to Lourdes very numerous spiritual and corporal graces. The ordinary channels of these graces are, with and in prayer, the ministry of priests at the Grotto (Confession, Eucharist, and the Anointing of the Sick), bathing in the waters, and the absorption of a little water from the miraculous source—this last practice may, of course, take place thousands of miles away from Lourdes.

Today, it is estimated that there have been a little more than 5,000 authentic cures since February 11, 1858, date of the first appearance of Our Lady. With great prudence and after long inquiries, the Church up to this time has declared as miraculous only about seventy of these. These modest numbers must not discourage us, because they concern only cures that can be scientifically established.

They in no way reflect the countless spiritual and corporal graces obtained by those who, in a difficult moment, have dared to turn with confidence to Our Lady of Lourdes. In the manner of the Memorare *(see p. 80), we could hold with good reason that no one has ever invoked the Immaculate Virgin in this way without quickly experiencing the help of her protection and her benefits.*

It is spurred on by this conviction that we now present the text of the Litany and a Novena dedicated to Our Lady of Lourdes. We will bear even greater witness of filial love for this good Mother if we accompany our prayer with a sip of the water that Mary recommended to Bernadette to drink and to have pilgrims drink.

Lord, have mercy.
Christ, have mercy.
Lord, have mercy.
Our Lady of Lourdes, Immaculate Virgin, pray for us.*
Our Lady of Lourdes, Mother of the Divine Redeemer,
Our Lady of Lourdes, who chose as your interpreter a weak and poor child,
Our Lady of Lourdes, who have caused to flow on earth a source that comforts so many pilgrims,

---

* *Pray for us* is recited after each invocation.

Our Lady of Lourdes, dispensatrix of the gifts of heaven,

Our Lady of Lourdes, to whom Jesus can refuse nothing,

Our Lady of Lourdes, whom no one has ever invoked in vain,

Our Lady of Lourdes, comforter of the afflicted,

Our Lady of Lourdes, who cure the sick,

Our Lady of Lourdes, hope of pilgrims,

Our Lady of Lourdes, who pray for sinners,

Our Lady of Lourdes, who invite us to repentance,

Our Lady of Lourdes, upholder of the holy Church,

Our Lady of Lourdes, advocate of the souls in purgatory,

Our Lady of Lourdes, Virgin of the most holy Rosary,

Lamb of God, You take away the sins of the world; *spare us, O Lord.*

Lamb of God, You take away the sins of the world; *graciously hear us, O Lord.*

Lamb of God, You take away the sins of the world; *have mercy on us.*

℣. Pray for us, Our Lady of Lourdes.

℟. *That we may be made worthy of the promises of Christ.*

Let us pray. Lord Jesus, we bless You and we thank You for all the graces that, through Your Mother at Lourdes, You pour down upon Your praying and suffering people. May we too, by the intercession of Our Lady of Lourdes, have a share in these benefits so that we may love You more and serve You better! ℟. *Amen.*

NOVENA TO OUR LADY OF LOURDES

Before each exercise proposed by the Novena, we should recite the Litany of Our Lady of Lourdes. (See p. 95.)

No matter how desperate the character of any situation may be, this Novena always obtains particular graces of strength and peace. However, we must realize that it is linked to some binding Christian acts. Therefore, it is better not to begin it unless we are resolved to carry out these practices as well as we can.

1st Day

Our Lady of Lourdes, Immaculate Virgin, pray for us.

Our Lady of Lourdes, here I am at your feet to ask for the following favor: . . . My confidence in your power of intercession is unshakable. You can obtain anything from your Divine Son.

Resolution: *Make an act of reconciliation in favor of some hostile person or someone from whom I have drawn away because of natural antipathy.*

2nd Day

Our Lady of Lourdes, who have chosen as your interpreter a weak and lowly child, pray for us.

Our Lady of Lourdes, help me to make use of all the means to become more humble and more reliant on God. I know that in this way I will be pleasing to you and obtain your assistance.

Resolution: *Choose an early date to go to confession and adhere to it.*

3rd Day

Our Lady of Lourdes, eighteen times blessed in your appearances, pray for us.

Our Lady of Lourdes, listen today to my supplicant requests. Grant them if by being carried out they will obtain the glory of God and the salvation of souls.

Resolution: *Make a visit to the Blessed Sacrament in a church. Entrust to Christ by name my loved ones, friends, and relatives who are in difficulty. Do not forget my dearly departed ones.*

4th Day

Our Lady of Lourdes, to whom Jesus can refuse nothing, pray for us.

Our Lady of Lourdes, intercede for me with your Divine Son. Fill your hands with the riches of His Heart and pour them forth on those who pray at your feet.

Resolution: *Recite today a meditative Rosary.*

5th Day

Our Lady of Lourdes, whom no one has ever invoked in vain, pray for us.

Our Lady of Lourdes, if you will it, none of those who are calling upon you today will leave without having experienced the effect of your powerful intercession.

Resolution: *This noon or this evening keep a partial fast in atonement for my sins as well as for the intentions of all those who are praying and will pray to Our Lady with this novena.*

6th Day

Our Lady of Lourdes, health of the sick, pray for us.

Our Lady of Lourdes, intercede for the sick whom we recommend to you. Obtain health for them, or at least an overabundance of strength.

Resolution: *Make a heartfelt act of consecration to Our Lady.* *

7th Day

Our Lady of Lourdes, who pray without ceasing for sinners, pray for us.

Our Lady of Lourdes, who led Bernadette to sanctity, grant me the Christian enthusiasm that does not shrink from any effort so that peace and love may reign more among human beings.

Resolution: *Visit a person who is sick or all alone.*

8th Day

Our Lady of Lourdes, maternal protector of the whole Church, pray for us.

---

*See, for example, the excellent text of Marian consecration by St. Louis Grignion de Montfort, p. 156.

Our Lady of Lourdes, protect our Pope and our bishop. Bless all the clergy and particularly the priests who make you known and loved. Remember all deceased priests who have transmitted to us the life of the soul.

Resolution: *Have a Mass celebrated for the souls in purgatory and receive Communion for this intention.*

9th Day

Our Lady of Lourdes, hope and consolation of pilgrims, pray for us.

Our Lady of Lourdes, at the end of this novena, I want to thank you for all the graces that you have obtained for me during the course of these days, and for those that you will yet obtain for me. In order the better to receive them and to thank you, I promise to try to come and pray to you in one of your shrines as soon as possible.

Resolution: *Once a year go in pilgrimage to a shrine of Mary, even one very close to my home, or make a spiritual retreat.*

INVOCATIONS UTTERED AT THE MOMENT OF BATHING IN THE WATERS OF LOURDES*

Blessed be the holy and immaculate Conception of the Blessed Virgin Mary, Mother of God.

Our Lady of Lourdes, pray for us.

My Mother, have pity on us.

Our Lady of Lourdes, heal us for the love and glory of the Blessed Trinity.†

Our Lady of Lourdes, heal us for the conversion of sinners.

Health of the sick, pray for us.

Help of the sick, pray for us.

O Mary conceived without sin, pray for us who have recourse to you.

St. Bernadette, pray for us.

---

*Here is a list of the invocations that were recited at the baths from 1930 to 1976. Afterward, one may prefer most often to say a prayer at choice such as the "Our Father." After the bath, one may recite the following two invocations: "Our Lady of Lourdes, pray for us" and "St. Bernadette, pray for us."

†An explicit request for a bodily healing is not contrary to the will of God and the Church. Father Tardiff, for example, declares: "Let the sick ask for their physical healing, for in this healing they always receive much more than a physical healing: they also receive a wonderful spiritual healing."

PRAYER OF JOHN PAUL II
FOR THE WORLD IN DANGER

O Mother of the human race and all peoples, help us to overcome the menace of evil that is so easily rooted in the hearts of people today and that, with its unequalled effects, weighs heavily on the lives of all and seems to close their eyes to the future!

From hunger and war, deliver us!

From nuclear war, an incalculable self-destruction, and all sorts of wars, deliver us!

From sins against human life from its first moments, deliver us!

From hatred and degradation for the dignity of the children of God, deliver us!

From all kinds of injustice in social, national, and international life, deliver us!

From the facile trampling underfoot of God's Commandments, deliver us!

From the attempt to stamp out of human hearts the very truth of God, deliver us!

From the loss of the knowledge of good and evil, deliver us!

From sins against the Holy Spirit, deliver us! Deliver us!

Hear, O Mother of Christ, this cry charged with the suffering of all human beings! Charged with the suffering of whole societies!

Help us, by the power of the Holy Spirit, to conquer all sin: the sin of human beings and the "sin of the world," sin under all its forms.

May there be revealed once again in the history of the world the infinite salvific power of the Redemption, the power of merciful Love! May it put a stop to Evil! May it transform consciences! May there be manifested in your Immaculate Heart the light of Hope for all!

Pope John Paul II on March 25, 1984 (extracts)

**ST. MICHAEL THE ARCHANGEL: OUR PRO-
TECTOR** — Like all the Angels, St. Michael the
Archangel is at the service of God and human
beings. We should pray often to this prince of
the heavenly host and defender of the Church.

6. PRAYERS TO THE ANGELS

Angels are mentioned in more than three hundred passages of Sacred Scripture. They are evoked there under diverse appellations, either individually or collectively. Their existence is wholly consecrated to the adoration and service of their Creator. For His salvific plans, God can at times send them to human beings in order to carry out various missions—imparting warning, protection, help, or instruction.

If we were more closely united with God dwelling in us, we would also be more sensitive to the active presence of these heavenly creatures. Moreover, if we knew how much they love us in God and can help us in His Name, we would think more often about greeting them and asking for their help and their beneficent inspirations.

Therefore, here are a few prayers that will enable us—especially in urgent cases—to better invoke our friends the Angels without neglecting the Angel that God has assigned as our "Guardian" to help us all along our earthly pilgrimage (see Exodus 23:20; Acts 12:15; Matthew 18:10).

INVOCATIONS TO THE
THREE ARCHANGELS

Glorious Archangel Michael, prince of the heavenly hosts, defend us against all our enemies both visible and invisible. Never permit that we fall under their cruel tyranny!

St. Gabriel the Archangel, you are called with good reason the strength of God, because you were chosen to announce to Mary the mystery in which the Almighty would have to deploy the power of His arm in a marvelous manner. Make us realize the treasures contained in the person of the Son of God, and be our messenger with His holy Mother!

St. Raphael the Archangel, charitable guide of voyagers, by the Divine power you work miraculous cures. Guide us on the course of our earthly pilgrimage and reveal to us the true remedies that can cure our souls and bodies. Amen.

TO ST. MICHAEL, AGAINST THE DEVIL

Holy Michael the Archangel, defend us in battle; be our safeguard against the wickedness and snares of the devil.

May God restrain him, we humbly pray; and you, prince of the heavenly host, by the power of God cast into hell Satan and all the evil spirits, who wander through the world seeking the ruin of souls. Amen.

INVOCATIONS TO OUR GUARDIAN ANGELS

Come to our assistance, O holy Angel Guardians. For you are helpers in our needs, consolers in our distress, illuminators in our darkness, protectors in dangers, inspirers of good thoughts, intercessors with God, bucklers repulsing the evil enemy, faithful companions, sure friends, prudent counselors, models of obedience, and mirrors of humility and purity.

Come to our assistance, O Angels who guard over us, Angels of our families, Angels of our children, the Angel of our parish, the Angel of our city, the Angel of our country, Angels of the Church, and Angels of the universe.

PRAYER TO OUR GUARDIAN ANGEL

Dear Angel of God who are my Guardian, enlighten, guide, and protect me! Never abandon me, even though I am a sinner. Take me by the hand and lead me to my goal along the holy paths of the love of God! Amen.

ANOTHER PRAYER TO OUR GUARDIAN ANGEL

O most faithful companion, appointed by God to be my guardian, and who never leave my side, how shall I thank you for your faithfulness and love and for the benefits you have obtained for me!

You watch over me when I sleep; you comfort me when I am sad; you avert the dangers that threaten me and warn me of those to come; you withdraw me from sin and inspire me to good; you exhort me to penance when I fall and reconcile me to God.

I beg you not to leave me. Comfort me in adversity, restrain me in prosperity, defend me in danger, and assist me in temptations, lest at any time I fall beneath them.

Offer up in the sight of the Divine Majesty my prayers and petitions, and all my works of piety, and help me to persevere in grace until I come to everlasting life. Amen.

INVOCATIONS TO THE NINE CHOIRS OF ANGELS

Most holy Angels, watch over us everywhere and forever.

Most noble Archangels, present to God our prayers and sacrifices.

Heavenly Virtues, give us strength and courage in time of trial.

Powers on high, defend us against our visible and invisible enemies.

Sovereign Principalities, govern our souls and our bodies.

Most elevated Dominations, rule over our humanity more and more.

Supreme Thrones, obtain peace for us.

Most zealous Cherubim, dissipate all our darknesses.

Most ardent Seraphim, enkindle in us a holy love for God.

ST. JOSEPH: PATRON OF THE CHURCH —
During his earthly life, St. Joseph was the foster father and protector of Jesus and Mary His Mother. Accordingly, Christians have called upon his aid unceasingly, and he has been named Patron of the Church of Jesus. He is the object of a devotion in the Church which has as its motto: "Go to Joseph."

7. PRAYERS TO THE SAINTS

PRAYER TO ST. JOSEPH TO ASK FOR HIS PROTECTION

We gain many graces by frequently asking for the intercession of this great Saint. The tradition of the Church places him among the greatest Saints. St. Teresa of Avila could not help acknowledging the following: "The Lord seems to have given grace to other Saints to assist us in one or other need; but St. Joseph, I know this by experience, helps us in all our needs. Our Lord doubtless wishes to show us by this that in heaven He hears all the prayers of the one to whom He was obedient on earth. . . .

"I would like to lead everybody to have devotion to this glorious Saint, since I have had so much experience of his credit with God!" (Life, ch. 6).

Blessed Joseph, by the tender affection that united you to the Immaculate Virgin, Mother of God, and by the fatherly love that you had for Jesus, I come to ask you to hear my urgent prayer.

O most wise guardian of the Holy Family, help me to keep my heart pure and generous. Assist me in the battles that I must wage against the Tempter. Just as you once saved the Infant Jesus from death, defend me today against the dangers that threaten my human life and my eternal salvation. Yes, grant me your powerful protection so that after your example and sustained by your aid, I may lead a holy life.

Good St. Joseph, obtain for me at last the grace of a happy death, in your company, with your Spouse and your Divine Son. Amen.

LITANY OF ST. JOSEPH

Lord, have mercy.
Christ, have mercy.
Lord, have mercy.
Christ, hear us.
Christ, graciously hear us.

God, the Father of heaven, *have mercy on us.*
God the Son, Redeemer of the world, *have mercy on us.*
God the Holy Spirit, *have mercy on us.*
Holy Trinity, one God, *have mercy on us.*

Holy Mary, *pray for us.* *
St. Joseph,
Renowned offspring of David,
Light of patriarchs,
Spouse of the Mother of God,
Chaste guardian of the Virgin,
Foster father of the Son of God,
Diligent protector of Christ,
Head of the Holy Family,
Joseph most just,
Joseph most chaste,
Joseph most prudent,
Joseph most strong,
Joseph most obedient,
Joseph most faithful,
Mirror of patience,
Lover of poverty,
Model of artisans,
Glory of home life,
Guardian of virgins,
Pillar of families,
Solace of the wretched,
Hope of the sick,
Patron of the dying,
Terror of demons,
Protector of Holy Church,

Pray for us is repeated after each invocation.

Lamb of God, you take away the sins of the world; *spare us, O Lord.*

Lamb of God, you take away the sins of the world; *graciously hear us, O Lord.*

Lamb of God, you take away the sins of the world; *have mercy on us.*

℣. He made him Lord of His household.
℟. *And prince over all His possessions.*

Let us pray. O God, in Your ineffable providence You were pleased to choose Blessed Joseph to be the spouse of Your most holy Mother. Grant, we beg You, that we may be worthy to have him for our intercessor in heaven whom on earth we venerate as our Protector: You who live and reign forever and ever. ℟. *Amen.*

STS. SIMON AND JUDE, PATRONS OF URGENT NEEDS

The devotion to Saint Jude the Apostle as patron of urgent and difficult cases seems to have taken wing after 1914 in Bavaria.

Undoubtedly some astounding grace was obtained in a parish dedicated to his name. In any case, people rapidly associated with his name that of St. Simon the Apostle, whose feast is also celebrated on October 28.

St. Simon, most zealous Apostle and ardent defender of the weak and the oppressed, your name signifies "God has heard." Since in our most difficult trials your intercession often obtains all kinds of unhoped for benefits, we come humbly to entrust ourselve to you, assured that God will be able once again to favorably receive your prayer and help us. We ask this through Jesus Christ, our Lord. Amen.

St. Jude, Apostle most attentive to the needs of our world (see John 14:22), whose name signifies "God be praised," come to teach us the true prayer that is pleasing to God. In our difficult situations, your intercession for us knows how to become pressing before the Lord. Thank you for coming to our aid in this way, dear Apostle, and teach us, even in the midst of our trials, to continue to praise the God of all goodness. We ask this through Jesus Christ, our Lord. Amen.

PRAYER TO ST. EXPEDITUS, PATRON OF URGENT CASES

We know very little about the life of St. Expeditus. According to the Roman Martyrology, *the Roman legionary Expeditus suffered martyr-*

dom for his faith on April 19, 303, in Armenia. Shortly after his death, his cult spread in Cappadocia, but it was only later that it passed on to Germany, Italy, and Spain. It entered France through the city of Pau, which still piously keeps his memory. The glorious Martyr is invoked today in numerous cities: Paris, Lyons, Lille, and Brussels, among others.

St. Expeditus is generally invoked for three reasons: to obtain success on examinations, since he is the Patron of Youth; to make intervention in urgent matters, since his name signifies "promptness"; and finally to intervene in cases of differences and disagreements, so that he may obtain the reconciliation of the parties.

O St. Expeditus, trusting in the promptness and power of your intercession, I ask you to intervene for me with the Lord. Here is the grace that I request: . . .

I am unworthy of any good, but I have confidence in you and in the Virgin Mary. May the Lord be pleased to answer her ardent prayer, and may He make me worthy of one day being able like you to shed my blood for love of Christ. Amen.

LITANY OF ST. EXPEDITUS

Lord, have mercy.

Christ, have mercy.

Lord, have mercy.

God, the Father of heaven, *have mercy on us.*

God the Son, Redeemer of the world, *have mercy on us.*

God the Holy Spirit, *have mercy on us.*

Holy Mary, *pray for us.**

St. Expeditus, glorious soldier of the Faith,

St. Expeditus, faithful even to death,

St. Expeditus, divested of everything out of love for Christ,

St. Expeditus, cruelly flogged,

St. Expeditus, courageously suffering death by the sword,

St. Expeditus, gloriously crowned in heaven,

St. Expeditus, patron of youth,

St. Expeditus, help of students,

St. Expeditus, model of soldiers,

St. Expeditus, protector of voyagers,

St. Expeditus, strength of the sick,

St. Expeditus, consoler of the afflicted,

St. Expeditus, mediator of lawsuits,

St. Expeditus, helper in urgent cases,

---

*Pray for us is said after every invocation.

St. Expeditus, model of dispatch,
St. Expeditus, support of your faithful
  friends,

Lamb of God, you take away the sins of the
  world; *spare us, O Lord.*
Lamb of God, you take away the sins of the
  world; *graciously hear us, O Lord.*
Lamb of God, you take away the sins of the
  world; *have mercy on us.*

Let us pray. Almighty Lord, through the
intercession of Your holy Martyr Expeditus, may our prayer be favorably received by You. May his protection gain for
us what our unworthiness could not merit.
We ask this through Your Son Jesus,
Strength of Martyrs and Redeemer of
human beings. ℟. *Amen.*

PRAYERS TO ST. RITA,
PATRONESS OF DESPERATE CASES

*St. Rita, a native Italian born in 1381, was
initially a saintly spouse, severely tested by the
violent nature of her husband. In 1416, he was
assassinated. She forgave his assassins and soon
took the veil among the Hermits of St. Augustine,
at Cascia.*

From 1441 until her death on May 22, 1457, she lived in prayer and astounding mystical sufferings. Her cult as Patroness of Desperate and Impossible Cases has spread all over the world, and the Church celebrates her feast on May 22.

In France, there is even a "St. Rita Association" (1 Rue de la Poissonnerie, Nice 06 300), which carries out various works under the Saint's patronage.

For a Particular Grace

O St. Rita, Saint of the Impossible and Advocate of Desperate Cases, I have recourse to you since I am engulfed by a trial.

Free my poor heart from the anguish that oppresses it and restore peace to my troubled spirit. You whom God has established as the Advocate of Desperate Cases, obtain for me the grace that I ask of you (*mention it here*). Shall I be the only one not to experience the efficacy of your powerful intercession?

If my sins constitute an obstacle to the fulfillment of my most cherished wishes, obtain for me the great grace of a sincere repentance and pardon through a good Confession. In any case, do not allow me to continue to live in such great affliction. Have pity on me!

O Lord, see the hope that I have in You! Listen to Your Blessed Rita who intercedes for us, the afflicted who are humanly without hope. Hear her prayers once more by manifesting Your mercy to us. Amen.

For a Sick Person

Most dear Heart of Jesus, with the same faith and the same love that dictated to Martha and Mary this appeal to You: "Lord, the one You love is sick!" I also dare to direct these words to You, for I ardently hope for the help of Your Divine mercy.

May Your grace, Lord Jesus, come through the hands of Your Most Holy Mother Mary and of Your servant Rita, so that the sick person whom I recommend may be brought back to health. Grant me this grace, O Lord, by the merits of Your faithful Rita. See her penances and her great pains that she suffered for 15 years by which You wished to unite her in a special way to Your Passion.

O St. Rita, intercede for me with your crucified Spouse. May He grant health to this sick person for whom I pray to you. It is through your special mediation that I await this grace. Convinced that it is God Himself Who inspires me to pray to you, I am certain that, through your merits, He will hear me in one manner or another for His greater glory. I believe it, I hope it, I am sure of it. I thank you in advance.

Glory be to the Father, and to the Son, and to the Holy Spirit. As it was in the beginning, is now, and ever shall be, world without end. Amen.

NOVENA TO ST. RITA

Recite the following prayers for nine successive days.

1st, 4th, and 7th Day

Most compassionate St. Rita, Advocate of Desperate Cases, consider with benevolence the prayers of an anguished heart and please obtain for me the grace that I need so much.

Our Father, Hail Mary, Glory Be.

2nd, 5th, and 8th Day

Most compassionate St. Rita, Advocate of Desperate Cases, I have recourse to you because I am certain of the power of your intercession. Please receive my request and present it to God yourself.

Our Father, Hail Mary, Glory Be.

3rd, 6th, and 9th Day

Most compassionate St. Rita, last recourse in urgent cases, I entrust myself to you with faith and love. In the situation that I have explained to you, you are my ultimate refuge. Have pity on me, through the Passion of Christ in which you shared so intimately!

Our Father, Hail Mary, Glory Be.

NOVENA TO ST. GERARD MAJELLA

Gerard Majella was born near Naples in 1726. An apprentice tailor, he was subjected to harsh treatment and frequent unmerited reproaches. He accepted everything with peace and patience, often repeating to himself the following words: "I desire at all costs to become a Saint, and I have the opportunity to do so. If I lose it, I lose it forever!"

In 1748, he joined the Redemptorists and rapidly attained an exceptional union with God. At his word, sinners became converted, the sick obtained health, and miracles were multiplied. He died on October 15, 1755. He is invoked most often for three intentions: as a guide and protector of young children; as a helper of mothers; and finally as the salvation of sinners.

For 9 consecutive days, recite a "Hail Mary" and the following prayer. If possible, make a Confession and receive Communion at the start of the Novena.

St. Gerard Majella, humble friar so powerful and so good, God seems to want to pour down on us through your hands the most varied of graces. Obtain for us the grace of corresponding better like you to the will of God, of being more faithful in praying to the Mother of the Redeemer, and—if Providence allows—of being relieved from all our ills.

O powerful protector, help of Christian families, strengthen the courage of mothers and preserve the souls and bodies of children.

For the sick, obtain health; for troubled hearts, peace; for guilty souls, pardon; for sinners, conversion; and for young people in search of their way, light about their vocation. For everybody, obtain an increase of generosity in the practice of the evangelical virtues, a constant fidelity to Christ and His Mother, and ultimately perseverance till death in the service of God. Amen.

NOVENA TO ST. THERESA OF THE CHILD JESUS FOR A CASE REPUTED TO BE DESPERATE

Born in Alencon in 1873, St. Theresa of the Child Jesus entered the Carmel of Lisieux at the age of fifteen and died there on September 30, 1897, consumed as much by love for God as by tuberculosis.

Heroically living the way of spiritual childhood, she was able in a few years' time to reach wondrous heights of a life of faith and hope. She remained faithful to God in the midst of the greatest darkness and—despite all kinds of moral and physical trials—succeeded in being attentive to her Sisters and to the missionary needs of the Church.

This magnificent little Saint, whose statue adorns many of our churches, is very often invoked in the most delicate and difficult cases. Catholics pray to her notably for the cure or alleviation of in-curable sicknesses; for the conversion of hardened sinners; for the consolation of persons strongly tempted by doubt and despair; for the deliverance of persecuted Christians; for the assistance of mis-sionaries; for the protection of persons threatened in one way or another; and for the souls of those who died without the aid of the Church. The graces ob-tained by her intercession are countless and solidly attested.

The following prayer should be said on nine con-secutive days, if possible before a statue or a photo of the Saint.

Dear little Theresa of the Child Jesus, great Saint of the pure love of God, I come today to entrust to you my ardent desire. Yes, very humbly, I come to ask your pow-erful intercession for the following grace: . . .

Shortly before your death, you asked God the favor of spending your heaven in doing good on earth. You even prophesied that you would pour down on us little ones a shower of roses. The Lord has heard your prayer: millions of pilgrims bear witness to it at Lisieux and throughout the whole world.

Bolstered by the certainty that you do not reject the lowly and afflicted, I come with confidence to ask for your help. Intercede for me with your crucified and glorified Spouse. Tell Him my desire. He will listen to you. He will listen to you as He listens to the Virgin Mary, for like her you never refused Him anything on earth.

Little Theresa, victim of love of the Lord, patroness of the missions, and model of simple and trusting souls, I address myself to you as to an older sister who is more powerful and more loving. Obtain for me the grace I seek if it is the will of God.

Blessed are you, little Theresa, for all the good that you have done for us and that you wish to continue to lavish on us until the end of the world. Yes, may you be a thousand times blessed and thanked for thus enabling us in some way to touch the goodness and mercy of our God! Amen.

PRAYER TO ST. ANTHONY OF PADUA

Born in Lisbon, Portugal, in 1195, St. Anthony is called "of Padua" because of his long residence in that Italian city. Priest and Doctor of the Church, he is venerated as one of the greatest Franciscan Saints. Devotion to this great Saint forms part of Catholic life in nearly every country of the world.

St. Anthony is known as a wonderworker because of his fame in obtaining miraculous favors from God. His reputation as a "finder of lost articles" assures us that evil and our daily misfortune have no lasting power over us since we have been redeemed by Christ—and that no request is too small for us to make of our heavenly friends, the Saints.

St. Anthony is also involved as a restorer of lost faith to those alienated from the Church and as a healer of both emotional and bodily sufferings.

St. Anthony, we come to entrust our pain to you. We know you as the worthy brother of St. Francis of Assisi. For God, you renounced riches and honors, you desired martyrdom, you preached to every creature and converted many sinners, and beginning in this life you obtained many miracles. Since God has given you such power in prayer when fulfilling our request can serve His glory, present our intention to Him yourself. Amen.

LITANY OF THE SAINTS
(Adapted)

Lord, have mercy.
Christ, have mercy.
Lord, have mercy.
Christ, hear us.
Christ, graciously hear us.
God, the Father of heaven, *have mercy on us.*
God the Son, Redeemer of the world, *have mercy on us.*
God the Holy Spirit, *have mercy on us.*

Holy Mary, *pray for us.*[*]
Holy Mother of God,
Holy Virgin of virgins,
Sts. Michael, Gabriel, and Raphael,
All you holy Angels of God,

St. Abraham,
St. Isaac and St. Jacob,
St. Joseph,
St. Moses,
St. David,
St. Job,
St. Isaiah and St. Jeremiah,
St. Elijah and St. Elisha,
St. John the Baptist,

---

[*] *Pray for us* is repeated after each invocation.

St. Joseph, Spouse of Mary,
All you holy Patriarchs and Prophets,

St. Peter and St. Paul,
St. Andrew,
St. John and St. James,
St. Thomas,
St. Matthew,
All you holy Apostles,

St. Luke and St. Mark,
St. Barnabas,
St. Mary Magdalene,
All you holy disciples of the Lord,

St. Stephen,
St. Ignatius of Antioch,
St. Polycarp of Smyrna,
St. Justin,
St. Pothinus and St. Blandina,
St. Irenaeus of Lyons,
St. Perpetua and St. Felicity,
St. Lawrence,
St. Cyprian of Carthage,
St. Agnes,
St. Thomas Becket,
St. Thomas More,
St. Maria Goretti,
St. Maximilian Kolbe.
All you holy Martyrs,

St. Leo the Great,
St. Gregory the Great,
St. Ambrose of Milan,
St. Jerome,
St. Augustine,
St. Athanasius of Alexandria,
St. Basil the Great,
St. Gregory Nazianzen,
St. John Chrysostom,
St. Hilary of Poitiers,
St. Martin of Tours,
St. Francis de Sales,
St. Pius X,
All you holy Bishops and Doctors,

St. Anthony of Egypt,
St. Benedict,
St. Bernard,
St. Francis of Assisi,
St. Anthony of Padua,
St. Dominic,
St. Thomas Aquinas,
St. Catherine of Siena,
St. Ignatius of Loyola,
St. Francis Xavier,
St. Teresa of Avila,
St. John of the Cross,
St. Rose of Lima,
St. Vincent de Paul,
St. John Mary Vianney,

St. Bernadette Soubirous,

St. John Bosco,

St. Theresa of the Child Jesus,

All you holy priests, religious men, and religious women,

St. Ann, Mother of Mary,

St. Monica,

St. Elizabeth of Hungary,

St. Elizabeth Ann Seton,

St. Frances Xavier Cabrini,

St. John Neumann,

St. Peter Claver,

All you Saints of God,

Lamb of God, You take away the sins of the world; *spare us, O Lord.*

Lamb of God, You take away the sins of the world; *graciously hear us, O Lord.*

Lamb of God, You take away the sins of the world; *have mercy on us.*

Let us pray. Father most holy, You know that without Your help we are all sinners. However, full of confidence in the merits of Your Son and the Saints, we beg You to make us worthy of the heavenly Kingdom that You have prepared for us from the foundation of the world. ℞. *Amen.*

THE HOLY SOULS: OUR INTERCESSORS —
The Church encourages us to pray for the
dead—either through liturgical prayers (like
the Eucharist and the Liturgy of the Hours) or
through private prayers (like those found in
this section). She also indicates that we may
ask the Holy Souls to intercede on our behalf.

8. PRAYERS TO THE SOULS IN PURGATORY

St. Catherine of Bologna (15th century) wrote: "When I desire to obtain a grace with certainty, I have recourse to the souls in purgatory, so that they may present my request to our common Father." This opinion is shared by numerous other spiritual persons, for example the saintly Curé of Ars (St. John Vianney) who said: "If only people knew how many graces we can obtain through the intercession of the souls in purgatory, they would not be so forgotten!"

There is no question here of falling into egotistic and useless calculations and spiritual exchanges such as: "I will pray to you if you give me!" Rather, it is a question of rediscovering an important dimension in the life of the Church, that Church which we call for want of something better the "suffering Church." Deceased Christians who have not yet been completely purified are possessed of great humility and consumed with a holy fervor for God and those who belong to Him. Because of this, they can profit from our prayers and merits but also intercede for us in a powerful way.

Therefore, let us not hesitate to ask for the help of these holy souls while at the same time praying ardently for them.

PRAYER OF ST. GERTRUDE

Dear Lord Jesus, I beg You, through the merits of Your most holy life, to hear this prayer that I address to You for all the dead of all time, and especially those for whom no one prays.

I ask that You supply for all that these souls neglected to do in the practice of Your praises, Your love, thanksgiving, prayer, virtues, and all the other good works that they could have done but never did or did too imperfectly. Amen.

PRAYER OF ST. ALPHONSUS LIGUORI

Most dear Jesus, by the bloody sweat that You experienced in Gethsemane, have mercy on these blessed souls!

Most dear Jesus, by the pains that You suffered in Your dolorous crowning with thorns, have mercy on these souls!

Most dear Jesus, by the pains that You suffered in carrying Your Cross up to Calvary, have mercy on these souls!

Most dear Jesus, by the pains that You suffered in Your most cruel crucifixion, have mercy on these souls!

Most dear Jesus, by the pains that You suffered in Your most bitter agony on the Cross, have mercy on these souls!

Most dear Jesus, by the immense pain that You suffered in dying misunderstood, rejected by everyone, and left all alone, have mercy on these souls!

PRAYER TO THE HOLY SOULS

Holy Souls of purgatory, may Jesus by His Precious Blood purify you completely and as soon as possible! I offer Him this good work or this sacrifice (*mention it*) so that He will move up, if possible, the time of your blessed birth in heaven.

At the same time, since I also am a poor sinner, I entrust the following intention to you: . . . Help me with your prayers! Thank you!

JESUS: OUR EXEMPLAR — During His agony in the Garden of Gethsemane (and later just before His Death on the Cross), Jesus entrusted Himself to the Heavenly Father in prayer. We should do the same.

9. ENTRUSTING OURSELVES TO GOD

Despite all our ardor and our faith, despite our perseverance and our multiple devotions that at times require real courage, it can happen that in view of a greater good that presently escapes us God wishes to hear our prayer in another way than the one we desire. It is then the time to reaffirm our trust. It is the time to throw ourselves into the arms of God with confidence, like a child. Here are a few texts that may help us do so.

THE EXEMPLARY WITNESS OF CHRIST

"Father, all things are possible to you. Take this cup away from me, but not what I will but what you will." Mark 14:36

"Father, into your hands I commend my spirit." Luke 23:46

PRAYER OF SELF-SURRENDER OF FATHER DE FOUCAULD

My Father, I surrender myself to You: do with me what You will. Whatever You do I thank You for it. I am ready for everything, and I accept everything, provided that Your will be done in me and in all Your creatures. I desire nothing else, O my God.

I entrust my soul into Your hands. I give it to You, my God, with all the love of my heart, because I love You, and it is a necessity of love for me to give myself, to entrust myself into Your hands without measure, with infinite confidence, for You are my Father.

PRAYER OF PASCAL TO ASK GOD FOR THE GOOD USE OF SICKNESS

Lord, Your spirit is so good and so gentle in all things. Grant me the grace not to act as a pagan in the state to which Your justice has reduced me. Let me as a good Christian acknowledge You as my Father and my God in whatever state I may find myself. For the change of my condition has no effect on Your state—You are always the same, and You are no less God when You afflict than when You console.

You have given me health to serve You, and I have (often) used it in a secular fashion. Now You send me sickness to correct me: do not allow me to use it to irk You by my impatience!

Take away from me, O Lord, the sadness that my love of self could cast over me because of my sufferings and because of the things of the world that do not succeed according to the inclinations of my heart. But place in me a sadness like Yours. May I henceforth desire neither health nor life except in order to use them and gear them for You, with You, and in You! I do not ask You for health, or sickness, or life, or death. I only ask that You use my health and my sickness, my life and my death, for Your glory, for my salvation, and for the good of the Church and the Saints.

Grant, O Lord, that I may conform myself to Your will and that sick as I am I may glorify You in my sufferings. Without them, I cannot attain heavenly glory, and You Yourself, my Savior, did not wish to come except through them. It is by the mark of Your sufferings that You were recognized by Your disciples, and it is by sufferings that You thus recognize who are

Your disciples. Recognize me, therefore, as Your disciple in the evils that I endure for the offenses that I have committed.

Unite my will to Yours and my pains to those that You have suffered. Grant that mine will become Yours. Unite me to Yourself. Fill me with Yourself and with Your Holy Spirit. Enter into my heart and my soul, to bring me my sufferings and to continue to endure in me what remains for You to suffer from Your Passion, which You complete in Your members until the perfect consummation of Your Body. Then, since I am filled with You, may it no longer be I who live and suffer, but You Who live and suffer in me, O my Redeemer!

Extract of sections I, II, XIII, XV

PRAYER OF SOMEONE NOT HEARD*

Lord, I asked You for health to be more effective on earth. You gave me weakness of body so that I would rely more on You than on myself.

Praised may you be, my God and Savior!

---

* Everyone can adapt this prayer in light of his or her own case. It is based on a celebrated prayer said to be composed by a Confederate soldier during the Civil War.

Lord, I asked You for a fine intelligence so that I might better understand the world and succeed in life. You gave me a struggling memory and a slow mind so that you might open Your mysteries to me through humility.

Praised may You be, my God and Savior!

Lord, I asked You for responsibilities so that I might bring about the triumph of good ideas and worthy causes. You gave me the grace of being treated as nothing and of being obedient to others so as to better configure me to Your obedient and crucified Son.

Praised may You be, my God and Savior!

Lord, I asked You that I might encounter a great love so as to give meaning to my life. You gave me the grace of being able to believe in the goodness of the human heart and the desire to share that faith with all the badly loved persons whom You made me meet.

Praised may You be, my God and Savior!

Lord, I asked You for riches so that I might help the poor. You gave me poverty and Your own riches to distribute.

Praised may You be, my God and Savior!

Lord, I asked You for a faith that would move mountains. You gave me the grace to have uneasy doubts that obliged me to remain prudent and totally abandoned to Your Providence.

Praised may You be, my God and Savior!

Lord, I asked You for the well-being of my dear ones. You gave them all kinds of trials, reminding me in this way that Jesus and His dear ones themselves suffered before entering into the joy of Your Kingdom.

Praised may You be, my God and Savior!

Lord, I asked You that I might become a Saint. You gave me the grace to see my sins better and to be able to rise after each of my grievous falls without despairing.

Praised may You be, my God and Savior!

PRAYER OF TOTAL CONFIDENCE

My God, not only do I have confidence in You, but I have no confidence except in You.

Give me, therefore, *the spirit of self-surrender* so that I may accept the things that I cannot change.

Give me also *the spirit of strength* so that I may change the things that I can change.

Lastly, give me *the spirit of wisdom* so that I may discern what depends effectively on me and may then do Your one and holy will! Amen.

Father Bernard-Marie
based on a thought of Marcus Aurelius

THE CURED LEPER: MODEL OF GRATITUDE —
Only one of ten lepers who received their cure
from Jesus came back to give Him thanks.
Jesus praised him for his action and indicated
that gratitude to God is a Christian virtue (Lk
17:11-19).

10. HOW TO THANK GOD

There is a scene in the Gospel that no person whose prayer has been heard should ever forget. It is the passage about the ten lepers to whom Jesus announces their cure if they go to the Temple out of faith in His word—considered ritually "unclean," they were strictly forbidden to enter the holy place. Having all been cured on the way, only one of the ten takes the time to retrace his steps to thank his Savior and bear witness to the power of God (see Luke 17:11-19).

We ourselves should take care not only to ask and receive but also to thank and bear witness. How can we do this? We can certainly recite or chant prayers of thanksgiving—and we will give examples below. However, as we said previously during the course of this book, God does not expect us to multiply words, and their value possesses no necessary and magical character.

We pray with our heart and our will and it is they who receive the Divine assistance of the Spirit; words are only modest supports that we must never make into absolutes. Without the Spirit that vivifies them, our most beautiful words directed toward heaven are only sweet illusions without deep and enduring practical consequences.

Therefore, if we have been heard in a truly providential manner, it is because our words have taken on flesh, blood, and spirit. It is because we have borne the risk of making a deep commitment—as much as our feeble faith will allow—to the holy words that we have uttered.

In this perspective, we will understand that the thanksgiving that pleases God most is constituted by all the acts that can bring us closer to His thrice holy Being and to our poorest and most deprived brothers and sisters in whom He hides.

Therefore, what will please God is every firmly kept resolution that will conform us a little more to the Christ of the Gospels. For example, the resolution:

● *to renounce a bad attitude or doubtful association;*

● *to practice greater fidelity to the daily duties of one's state;*

● *to go to Confession and receive Communion more frequently;*

● *to consecrate at least ten minutes a day to prayer;*

● *to reserve from time to time a little moment at night to intercede for sinners as Jesus did in Gethsemane;*

● *to actively practice the forgiveness of offenses by initiating an act of reconciliation even though we are the injured party;*

● *to regularly help a humanitarian organization;*

● *to visit the isolated, the afflicted, the sick, prisoners, and the aged;*

● *to go on a pilgrimage or make a retreat annually;*

● *to read the Bible every day and foster its distribution;*

● *to bear witness as often as possible to the Good News dwelling in us;*

● *and to carry out similar practices.*

Once we have begun to act according to what the Spirit inspires in us, we can then lift up our chant of gladness.

We will cite here only a few examples, which are but extracts.

PSALM 148

Praise the Lord from the heavens,
    praise him from the heights;
Praise him, all you his angels,
    praise him, all you his hosts.
Praise him, sun and moon;
    praise him, all you shining stars.

Let them praise the name of the Lord,
  for he commanded and they were
    created.
Young men too, and maidens,
  old men and boys.
Praise the name of the Lord,
  for his name alone is exalted;
His majesty is above earth and heaven,
  and he has lifted up the horn of his peo-
    ple.
Be this his praise from all his faithful ones,
  from the children of Israel, the people
    close to him. Alleluia.

(Verses 1-3, 5, 12-14)

See also Psalms 67; 111; 116.

CANTICLE OF THE THREE YOUNG MEN IN THE FURNACE

Bless the Lord, all you works of the Lord,
  praise and exalt him above all forever.
Angels of the Lord, bless the Lord,
  praise and exalt him above all forever.
Sun and moon, bless the Lord;
  praise and exalt him above all forever.
Stars of heaven, bless the Lord;
  praise and exalt him above all forever.
Nights and days, bless the Lord;
  praise and exalt him above all forever.

Everything growing from the earth, bless
the Lord;
praise and exalt him above all forever.
You dolphins and all water creatures, bless
the Lord;
praise and exalt him above all forever.
All you birds of the air, bless the Lord;
praise and exalt him above all forever.
All you beasts, wild and tame, bless the
Lord;
praise and exalt him above all forever.
You sons of men, bless the Lord;
praise and exalt him above all forever.

(Verses 57-58, 62-63, 71, 76, 79-82)

CANTICLE OF MARY OR "MAGNIFICAT"

My soul proclaims the greatness of the
Lord;
my spirit rejoices in God my savior.
For he has looked upon his handmaid's
lowliness. . . .
The Mighty One has done great things for
me,
and holy is his name.
His mercy is from age to age
to those who fear him.

(Luke 1:46-50)

HYMN OF THANKSGIVING
OR "TE DEUM"

You are God: we praise You;
You are the Lord: we acclaim You;
You are the eternal Father:
All creation worships You.

To You all angels, all the powers of
heaven,
Cherubim and Seraphim, sing in endless
praise:
  Holy, holy, holy, Lord, God of power
  and might,
  heaven and earth are full of Your glory.

The glorious company of Apostles praise
You.
The noble fellowship of Prophets praise
You.
The white-robed army of Martyrs praise
You.

Throughout the world the holy Church
acclaims You:
  Father of majesty unbounded,
  Your true and only Son, worthy of all
  worship,
  and the Holy Spirit, advocate and guide.

You, Christ, are the King of glory,
the eternal Son of the Father.

When You became man to set us free
You did not spurn the Virgin's womb.

You overcame the sting of death,
and opened the kingdom of heaven to all
   believers.

You are seated at God's right hand in
   glory.
We believe that You will come, and be our
   judge.

Come then, Lord, and help Your people,
bought with the price of Your own Blood,
and bring us with Your Saints
to glory everlasting.

℣. Save Your people, Lord, and bless
   Your inheritance.
℟. *Govern and uphold them now and always.*
℣. Day by day we bless You.
℟. *We praise Your name forever.*
℣. Keep us today, Lord, from all sin.
℟. *Have mercy on us, Lord, have mercy.*
℣. Lord, show us Your love and mercy.
℟. *for we put our trust in You.*
℣. In You, Lord, is our hope:
℟. *and we shall never hope in vain.*

SIMPLE THANK YOU'S

Lord, thank You for creating me!
Lord, thank You for redeeming me!
Lord, thank You for giving me faith!
Lord, thank You for giving Yourself to me!
Lord, thank You for hearing me!
Lord, thank You for granting my request!
Lord, thank You for remaining with me,
  with him, with her,
  with us, with them,
forever, for You are Love! Amen.

IN THANKSGIVING TO OUR LADY*

O Mary, I choose you today in the presence of the whole court of heaven as my Mother and Queen. I offer and consecrate to you, with total submission and love, my body and my soul, my interior and exterior

---

*We leave the reader with one of the most beautiful consecrations to Mary. There are, however, a number of prayers and novenas of supplication that we have not cited here. We were forced to make a choice and we opted for the greatest diversity and spiritual richness possible combined with brevity. Nonetheless, we will gratefully receive every proposal that would further enrich the minimum foundation given here.

goods, and even the value of my past, present, and future good works. I give you the complete and full right to dispose of myself and of everything that belongs to me without exception, in accord with your good pleasure, for the greater glory of God in time and eternity. Amen.

St. Louis Grignion de Montfort

THEMATIC TABLE OF INTENTIONS*

*To facilitate the use of this book, we have grouped here a certain number of intentions, but these thematic groupings are no more than simple suggestions and not obedient to any necessary or "magical" character. We repeat once more: God alone is the Master of the Impossible and ultimate Judge of what is best for us. Even if we "deceive" ourselves with an intermediary, our prayer will reach Him, for He is a Father and Love!

For Safeguarding or Reestablishing Peace

Litany of the Holy Passion of Christ, 58
The Rosary, 77
Rosary of the Divine Mercy, 41
Litany of the Sacred Heart of Jesus, 43
Litany of the Holy Spirit, 72
Litany of the Blessed Virgin Mary, 82
Prayer of John Paul II for the World, 106
Prayers to the Angels, 109
Litany of the Saints, 132

In Case of Family Problems (Search for Unity, Fecundity, Means of Subsistence, Protection of Children, etc.)

Psalm 22, 20
Psalm 130, 22
Psalm 25, 23
Prayer of St. Augustine, 29
For Peace in Families, 30
Novena of Trust in the Heart of Christ, 42
Litany of the Sacred Heart of Jesus, 43
Litany of the Holy Spirit, 72
The Rosary, 77
Novena to Our Lady of Perpetual Help, 87
Prayer to St. Joseph, 115
Litany of St. Joseph, 116
Prayer to and Litany of St. Expeditus, 119-121
Novena to St. Gerard Majella, 126

In Case of Invincible Temptations or Grave Evil Attitudes

Litany of the Holy Spirit, 72
The Rosary, 77
The "Memorare," 80
Novena to Our Lady of Perpetual Help, 87

Novena to Our Lady of Lourdes, 100
Prayers to the Angels, 109
Prayer to St. Joseph, 115
Novena to St. Theresa of the Child Jesus, 128
Litany of the Saints, 132

For Enlightenment (Important Decision, Vocation, Choice for One's Whole Life, Examen, etc.)

Psalm 25, 23
Litany of the Holy Spirit, 72
The Rosary, 77
Litany of the Blessed Virgin Mary, 82
Novena to Our Lady of Perpetual Help, 87
Novena to Our Lady of Lourdes, 100
Prayers to the Angels, 109
Prayer to and Litany of St. Expeditus, 119-121
Novena to St. Gerard Majella, 126
Litany of the Saints, 132

Prayers of Abandonment and Consecration

Act of Hope (of Father Engel), 30
The Exemplary Witness of Christ, 141
Prayer of Self-Surrender of Father de Foucauld, 141
Prayer of Pascal, 142
Prayer of Someone Not Heard, 144
Consecration to Our Lady, 156

Prayers of Thanksgiving

Psalm 148, 151
Canticle of Three Young Men, 152
Canticle of Mary or "Magnificat," 153
Hymn of Thanksgiving or "Te Deum," 154
Simple Thank You's, 156
In Thanksgiving to Our Lady, 156